LOVE'S COMEDY

BY HENRICK IBSEN

TRANSLATED AND WITH AN INTRODUCTIONBY C. H. HERFORD

INTRODUCTION

Love's Comedy is without doubt the finest of the few plays of Ibsen which still remain inaccessible to the English reader. It belongs, like *Brand* and *Peer Gynt*, to the early noontide of his genius, and exhibits in a cruder form, that union of philosophic reflection with the happy valiancy and abounding resource of youth, which is the special grace of the early thirties. To the reader of the "Social Dramas," and especially to the reader who has enjoyed their subject-matter but resented their studied banality of form, *Love's Comedy* should be highly congenial; for it handles a kindred theme with radiant vivacity and verve, and presents, through a medium charged with eloquence and imagery, a picture not less dramatic and alive, of the same society. Ibsen had here, in fact, struck for the first time the rich vein which the last thirty years of his life have been devoted to working out; and he hewed it with ringing strokes in the first ardour of discovery. *Love's Comedy* marks the true inception of the "Social Dramas"; it may even be held to contain them in the germ.

I

Kærlighedens Komedie was produced at Christiania in 1862. The polite world—so far as such a thing existed at that time in the Northern capital—received it with an outburst of indignation not now entirely easy to understand. It has indeed faults enough. The character-drawing is often crude, the action, though full of effective by-play, extremely slight, and the sensational climax has little relation to human nature as exhibited in Norway, or out of it, at that or any other time. But the sting lay in the unflattering veracity of the piece as a whole; in the merciless portrayal of the trivialities of persons, or classes, high in their own esteem; in the unexampled effrontery of bringing a clergyman upon the stage. All these have long since passed, in Scandinavia, into the category of the things which people take with their Ibsen as a matter of course, and the play is welcomed with delight by every Scandinavian audience. But in 1862 the matter was serious, and Ibsen meant it to be so.

For they were years of ferment—those six or seven which intervened between his return to Christiania from Bergen in 1857, and his departure for Italy in 1864. As director of the newly founded "Norwegian Theatre," Ibsen was a prominent member of the little knot of brilliant young writers who led the nationalist revolt against Danish literary tradition, then still dominant in well-to-do, and especially in official, Christiania. Well-to-do and official Christiania met the revolt with contempt. Under such conditions, the specific literary battle of the Norwegian with the Dane easily developed into the eternal warfare of youthful idealism with "respectability" and convention. Ibsen had already started work upon the greatest of his Norse Histories—*The Pretenders to the Crown*. But history was for him little more than material for the illustration of modern problems; and he turned with zest from the task of breathing his own spirit into the stubborn mould of the thirteenth century, to hold up the satiric mirror to the suburban drawing-rooms of Christiania, and to the varied phenomena current there,—and in suburban drawing-rooms elsewhere,—under the name of Love.

Yet *Love's Comedy* is much more than a satire, and its exuberant humour has a bitter core; the laughter that rings through it is the harsh, implacable laughter of Carlyle. His criticism of commonplace love-making is at first sight harmless and ordinary enough. The ceremonial formalities of the continental *Verlobung*, the shrill raptures of aunts and cousins over the engaged pair, the satisfied smile of enterprising materfamilias as she reckons up the tale of daughters or of nieces safely married off under her auspices; or, again, the embarrassments incident to a prolonged *Brautstand* following a hasty wooing, the deadly effect of familiarity upon a shallow affection, and the anxious efforts to save the appearance of romance when its zest has departed—all these things had yielded such "comedy" as they possess to many others before Ibsen, and an Ibsen was not needed to evoke it. But if we ask what, then, is the right way from which these "comic" personages in their several fashions diverge; what is the condition which will secure courtship from ridicule, and marriage from disillusion, Ibsen abruptly parts company with all his predecessors. "'Of course,' reply the rest in chorus, 'a deep and sincere love';—'together,' add some, 'with prudent good sense.'" The prudent good sense Ibsen allows; but he couples with it the startling paradox that the first condition of a happy marriage is the absence of love, and the first condition of an enduring love the absence of marriage.

INTRODUCTION

The student of the latter-day Ibsen is naturally somewhat taken aback to find the grim poet of Doubt, whose task it seems to be to apply a corrosive criticism to modern institutions in general and to marriage in particular, gravely defending the "marriage of convenience." And his amazement is not diminished by the sense that the author of this plea for the loveless marriage, which poets have in all times scorned and derided, was himself beyond question a poet, ardent, brilliant, and young, and himself, what is more, quite recently and beyond question happily, married. The truth is that there are two men in Ibsen:—an idealist, exalted to the verge of sentimentality, and a critic, hard, inexorable, remorseless, to the verge of cynicism. What we call his "social philosophy" is a *modus vivendi* arrived at between them. Both agree in repudiating "marriage for love"; but the idealist repudiates it in the name of love, the critic in the name of marriage. Love, for the idealist Ibsen, is a passion which loses its virtue when it reaches its goal, which inspires only while it aspires, and flags bewildered when it attains. Marriage, for the critic Ibsen, is an institution beset with pitfalls into which those are surest to step who enter it blinded with love. In the latter dramas the tragedy of married life is commonly generated by other forms of blindness—the childish innocence of Nora, the maidenly ignorance of Helena Alving, neither of whom married precisely "for love"; here it is blind Love alone who, to the jealous eye of the critic, plays the part of the Serpent in the Edens of wedded bliss. There is, it is clear, an element of unsolved contradiction in Ibsen's thought;—Love is at once so precious and so deadly, a possession so glorious that all other things in life are of less worth, and yet capable of producing only disastrously illusive effects upon those who have entered into the relations to which it prompts. But with Ibsen—and it is a grave intellectual defect — there is an absolute antagonism between spirit and form. An institution is always, with him, a shackle for the free life of souls, not an organ through which they attain expression ; and since the institution of marriage cannot but be, there remains as the only logical solution that which he enjoins —to keep the soul's life out of it. To " those about to marry," Ibsen therefore says in effect : " Be sure you are not in love ! " And to those who are in love he says : " Part ! "

It is easy to understand the irony with which a man who thought thus of love contemplated the business of "love-making," and the ceremonial discipline of Continental courtship. The whole unnumbered tribe of wooing and plighted lovers were for him unconscious actors in a world-comedy of Love's contriving—naïve fools of fancy, passionately weaving the cords that are to strangle passion. Comedy like this cannot be altogether gay ; and as each fresh romance decays into routine, and each aspiring passion goes out under the spell of a vulgar environment, or submits to the bitter salvation of a final parting, the ringing laughter grows harsh and hollow, and notes of ineffable sadness escape from the poet's Stoic self-restraint.

II

Ibsen was not the first Norwegian who derided the humours of love. To his earliest readers his play recalled a famous novel, Camilla Collet's *The Official's Daughters*, which had, since 1857, greatly exercised the Scandinavian world. The novel anticipated the play in its vigorous attack upon the current usages of courtship and marriage. But Fru Collet's quarrel with them rested on wholly different grounds. With her, the trouble lay in the restrictions imposed by social usage upon the free course of love. She pleaded for the right of woman to bestow her heart where she would. She belonged, in fact, to a mild variety of the revolutionary Romantic, for whom love is the sole condition of happiness, and outward control the only source of danger to love. Marriage for love was her last word. For Ibsen, as we have seen, this was the very disease to be combated. He derided the ceremonious conventionalities of fashionable love-making as trenchantly as she; not, however, because they suppressed or constrained love, but because they gave it organised expression and definite form. At bottom, his position was not so much the antithesis of hers, as its extreme development. He too is a revolutionary Romantic, whose last words are emancipation and love. Only, his "emancipation" of love is so transcendent as to threaten to "emancipate" it from the very conditions of its material existence. His freedom is only fulfilled when the captive is delivered from the thraldom of blood and breath; when it escapes the "prison of the actual," and dies that it may live.

In his interesting introduction to this play in the German edition of Ibsen's works (Berlin: Fischer, 1899), George Brandes, who first discussed its relation to Fru Collet's novel, has criticised the *dénoûment* with much severity. Falk and Svanhild part because they have not confidence that their love will last, if they marry. As he justly observes, that does not happen in the world we know. It belongs to Ibsen's ideal world, and is perfectly in keeping with the axioms and prejudices there current. While recognising this, however, he uses language which suggests that it is after all a very ordinary, not to say vulgar, affair indeed. To Falk's passionate claim that their love is not as the love of common lovers, that it can resist the corrosive influences of married life, she makes what Brandes calls this "improbable and truly philistine reply"—

> "But if Love, notwithstanding should decay,
> Love being Happiness's single stay—
> Could you avert, then, Happiness's fall?" (p. 153).

To which Falk answers:

> "No, my love's ruin were the wreck of all."

"How can she," comments Brandes, "imagine for herself and for Falk, a happiness founded upon anything but mutual love? Ibsen, however, chose to make her so imagine, and thus we see her subside with her eyes open into the arms of Guldstad, who offers her a maintenance, a peaceful home, and ample means." With all deference, however, to so distinguished a critic, it may be insisted that she imagines nothing of the kind. Happiness *is*, for her, to be had only through love. She implies nothing at variance with that faith when she asks if he has any means to happiness, in love's default—as she might have asked whether he had any means of seeing, if his eye-sight gave way. The desire for happiness, as ordinarily understood, has nothing whatever to do with her decision. The passion which animates it is not the love of happiness but the love of *Love*. True, a kind of happiness is always involved when a supreme passion has its way; the Stoic wise man claimed to be peculiarly "happy" on the rack, the Christian martyr exulted in his aureole of glory at the stake. But obviously these rare and transcendent forms of happiness have little to do with the dreams of a comfortable home and plenty of pin-money, which lure Dr Brandes' practical young bourgeoise Svanhild to her choice. And it is the martyr's happiness alone which Ibsen's Svanhild knows. The happiness of union with Falk she surrenders in order to retain the undimmed splendour of their love. "We have had our joy," she tells him; "the vessel of our fate is wrecked; but one plank still floats, and bold swimmers may yet reach their Paradise; let Happiness sink and be drowned, our Love shall yet, thank God, be borne in triumph to the shore" (p. 155). Her language about love is, it is true, at first sight glaringly inconsistent as well as paradoxical. Here it is said to survive when Happiness perishes; a score of lines before she had said (p. 154) that their love should *die*—in the fulness of its glorious youth, untainted by sickness or age. The clue to these apparent anomalies lies in Ibsen's idealisation of remembered existence. "Nothing abides but the Lost," is the heroic faith which nerves Brand in the agony of Agnes' last "good-night." And Love, in order to truly live, has, for Ibsen, to undergo a death-like rupture with the world of matter and sensation, and to pass into a transfigured spiritual existence, pure and intense as "remembered kisses after death." This is the thought of which Falk catches the inspiration when Svanhild's meaning at length bursts upon him—

"Now I divine!
Thus and no otherwise canst thou be mine!

INTRODUCTION

> As the grave opens into Life's Dawn fire,
> So Love with Life may not espoused be
> Till, loosed from longing and from wild desire,
> It soars into the heaven of memory!
> Pluck off the ring!"

This passionate idealism which invests the phantoms of memory with the attributes of supreme reality is necessarily puzzling to persons accustomed to read in their newspapers of the sordid realist Ibsen, who paints things *as they are.* A few years later, he characteristically gave to those survivals of dead men in their evil deeds, which had never before been clothed in a semblance so horribly vital, the appalling name of Ghosts. Ibsen's idealism has, at this stage, much affinity to that distrust and disparagement of attainment, completion, fixity, with which we are familiar in Browning and in Carlyle. This strange unearthly "love" of his — in which, as Brandes finely says, "Norse coldness, rigour, enthusiasm, and ascetic disdain for the senses are mingled,"—has points of analogy to the divine "thirst" of the "infinite shoeblack" in *Sartor*, whom oceans of Hochheimer cannot satisfy; to the "aspiration" of Paracelsus, who is great when he aspires, and fails when he attains. But Ibsen's criticism of actuality is yet more thoroughgoing and more bitter than Carlyle's; while the buoyant, irrepressible confidence in the working of all things for good, which pervades Browning, is wholly foreign to the terrible poet of the North. It is characteristic of their diversity of temper that, to the state of satisfied attainment, which both disparage, Browning opposes, as the state of supreme well-being, aspiration with its exalted hopes, Ibsen memory, with its meditative retrospect. But Browning's gospel of aspiration has its roots in psychological analysis and theological prepossession; while Ibsen's canonisation of memory is grounded altogether on his social or anti-social instincts—on his abhorrence of the organised community, great and small, his fixed persuasion of the disastrous effect upon its members of active participation in its life. To the myriads of "the church" or of "the state," as to the myriad married pairs, he allows the banality of sensation and satisfied passion, reserving the lovely ecstacies of memory for "the strong man who stands alone."

The strength of loneliness may fairly be called the central *motif* of Ibsen's work. Even in the special form which inspired *Love's Comedy*—the strength of lonely love—it had haunted him from youth. At twenty-one, an age not particularly alive, as a rule, to the raptures of abnegation in love, he had already imagined a parallel to the parting of Falk and Svanhild. Henrik Jæger, his biographer, describes among a series of early MS. pieces written between nineteen and twenty-two, a poem called "Recollections of a ball: a fragment of life in verse and prose." At the ball the poet meets a young girl—the fulfilment, he thinks, of all he had dreamed of in the woman he would one day love. He loses himself in the intoxication of her presence: "What is a life of struggle and disillusion compared to a half-hour like this?" But that is enough. "Fate! take from me this overwhelming bliss, do not desecrate this moment byprolonging it. I have had it—what would I more?" And fate listens: he hears that she is engaged. But her memory remains his spiritual possession.* And Brandes has pointed out how even the

* Jæger: *Henrik Ibsen*, 1828-1888. Brandes *u.s.*, p. xvi., from whom I borrow the description.

fierce Valkyrie-like Hjördis in the *Vikings*—the very embodiment of the implacable Germanic love which will have its way—has to drink the cup of ascetic idealism tendered by her creator, and to cry to Sigurd at the point of death: "O it is better so than if thou hadst wedded me here in this life—if I had sat in thy homestead weaving linen and wool for thee and bearing thee children—pah!" It is not for nothing, we see, that Svanhild has her heroic name, and her vision of the wild ride upon the savage horse of Eormenric; her eyes, too, are strangely expressive, like those which, according to the Edda, struck awe into the horses that were to trample to death her Volsung namesake, so that they would not touch her till someone covered her face.

The conviction of the strength of loneliness dominates the work which followed, as well as that which preceded, our play. But the note of ecstatic fervour is less often heard. In *Brand*, indeed, it even gathers volume and intensity; Svanhild's rapture of renunciation is resumed with heightened tragic power in the great transfiguration of the tortured mother who has broken her last idol.* But in the prose dramas the ecstatic note grows less distinct and assured; and while the man who stands alone is still the dominating theme, his more transcendental compensations are rescinded, the problems which confront him grow more complex, the web of circumstance which invests him more subtle and treacherous; his errors and collapses are scornfully travestied, as in Gregers Werle; and at times, as in *Ghosts*, we are made to face, in its most

* For another close parallel compare *Love's Comedy*, p. 59 (Falk and Svanhild), with Brand's words as Agnes enters with the Christmas candles (Act iv., p. 164, in my version.)

appalling form, the implacable tyranny of the past, and to ask with a shudder: "Who then *can* stand alone?"

III

Yet the reminiscences of the heroic legends of Norway which Ibsen had recently explored to so much purpose, must not be pressed too far. Svanhild is shaped after the mould of the modern world (p. 59); and the purely literary influences disclosed in the play point to quite other sources than the sagas. Between the sinewy classic prose of Iceland and the romantic and picturesque vivacity of the prose of Heine lies an interval as wide as is to be found in literature between two manners both of supreme excellence; yet both held sway in the literary workshops of young Norway. Ibsen's earliest and most brilliant elder associates, Paul Botten-Hansen and A. O. Vinje, were steeped in Heine, though Vinje, at least, one of the most original and fascinating of all Norwegian poets, invaded him royally, and made his own what he took. His *Ferdaminni* ("Reise-erinnerungen") is a kind of Norwegian *Reisebilder*, as rich in poetry if not in wit, as its prototype. He also edited a journal (*Dölen*, "The Dalesman") which obtained great fame throughout Norway and procured him the title as a soubriquet. Hansen had written an essay on Young Germany, and a novel, *Norske Mysterier*, the style of which, "thridded with biting and disintegrating reflection, and scattered with allusion and quotation," is palpably Heinesque. Both Hansen and Vinje receive passing mention in highly honourable terms in our play. Hansen is the "gray old stager" of p. 20; the saying attributed to him is, in the original, a literal quotation from an epigram of his—

> "thi Kjærligheden gjör Petrarker,
> som Fæ og Ladhed Patriarker."

The law-clerk Stiver has also been thought to be modelled on Hansen's Jurist Karlsen in his play *Huldrebryllupet.* Vinje is referred to on p. 135 as *Dölen*; where, however, I have substituted an allusion more familiar to the English ear.

Ibsen had thus grown up in a school which cultivated the romantic, piquant, picturesque in style; which ran riot in wit, in vivacious and brilliant imagery, in resonant rhythms and telling double rhymes. It must be owned that this was not the happiest school for a dramatist, nor can *Love's Comedy* be regarded, in the matter of style, as other than a risky experiment which nothing but the sheer dramatic force of an Ibsen could have carried through. As it is, there are palpable fluctuations, discrepancies of manner; the realism of treatment often provokes a realism of style out of keeping with the lyric afflatus of the verse; and we pass with little warning from the barest colloquial prose to strains of high-wrought poetic fancy. Nevertheless, the style, with all its inequalities, becomes in Ibsen's hands a singularly plastic medium of dramatic expression. The marble is too richly veined for ideal sculpture, but it takes the print of life. The wit, exuberant as it is, does not coruscate indiscriminately upon all lips; and it has many shades and varieties—caustic, ironical, imaginative, playful, passionate—which take their temper from the speaker's mood.

For the rest, the play has obviously suffered, as a play, from the vigour of its satiric animus. Satirist and dramatist here entered upon a life-long partnership; and the satirist was the leading partner, and determined the policy of the firm,—a privilege which he was never again in anything like the same measure to enjoy. The dramatist had to provide living victims for the satirist to bruise and maul; he had also to intervene, like the surgeon at a duel, when there is danger of his bruising them to death. But in one or two cases, it must be owned, the combative partner has done his business quite undisturbed. Mrs Strawman is not a person, but a galvanised corpse. The satirist has bruised her out of existence.

The present version of the play retains the metre of the original. The sequence of rhymes is there arbitrary, and the same arbitrariness has been allowed, in most cases, to determine their sequence in the translation. Undertaken some time ago, it has been carried on in the intervals of more pressing work, and more than once abandoned altogether. The work was still incomplete when a very exacting literary engagement compelled me to put it for some months aside, and it would not be published now had I not, through the generous kindness of Mr William Archer, been enabled to use an admirable fragment of his own. The reader will turn with interest to this specimen of the metrical accomplishment of a past master of Norwegian lore, whose eminence as a critic of poetry and of drama needs no recognition here. It forms the opening scene of the drama, ending at page 20. In this passage only about a dozen scattered lines are mine. Two other passages, substantially my own — Falk's tirades on pp. 58 and 100—contain a few lines from Mr Archer's independent version. My collaborator, as I may thus fairly call him, declined to allow his name to appear on the title-page; but while I feel reluctance in ostensibly claiming as entirely my own a book into which another man has put his wit, I shall not apologise to the reader for bringing better luck in his way than the title-page gave him a right to expect. Some two or three lines have also been taken from the extracts translated by Mr Gosse in the English version of Jæger's biography; and about as many more owe something in the way of suggestion to the same source.

I would also present my acknowledgments to the editor and publishers of the *Fortnightly Review* for their kindness in permitting me to reprint portions of an article contained in the current (February) number. In conclusion I would refer any of my readers who do not know it to the admirable discussion of this play, on its ethical side, by Mr P. H. Wicksteed in his *Four Lectures on Ibsen* (Sonnenschein)—a discussion to which my own owes much.

LOVE'S COMEDY

PERSONS OF THE COMEDY

Mrs Halm, *widow of a government official.*
Svanhild, } *her daughters.*
Anna, }
Falk, *a young author,* } *her boarders.*
Lind, *a divinity student,* }
Guldstad, *a wholesale merchant.*
Stiver, *a law-clerk.*
Miss Jay, *his fiancée.*
Strawman, *a country clergyman.*
Mrs Strawman, *his wife.*
Students, Guests, Married and Plighted Pairs.
The Strawmans' Eight Little Girls.
Four Aunts, a Porter, Domestic Servants.

Scene—*Mrs Halm's Villa on the Drammensvejen at Christiania.*

ACT I

The SCENE *represents a pretty garden irregularly but tastefully laid out; in the background are seen the fjord and the islands. To the left is the house, with a verandah and an open dormer window above; to the right in the foreground an open summer-house with a table and benches. The landscape lies in bright afternoon sunshine. It is early summer; the fruit-trees are in flower.*

(*When the Curtain rises,* MRS HALM, ANNA *and* MISS JAY *are sitting in the verandah, the first two engaged in embroidery, the last with a book. In the summer-house are seen* FALK, LIND, GULDSTAD, *and* STIVER: *a punch-bowl and glasses are on the table.* SVANHILD *sits alone in the background by the water.*)

FALK (*rises, lifts his glass, and sings*).

Sun-glad day in garden shady
  Dawns for thy delight alone;
What though promises of May-day
  Chilly autumn oft disown?
Apple-blossom white and splendid
  Drapes thee in its glowing tent,—
Let it, then, when day is ended,
  Strew the closes storm-besprent.

CHORUS OF GENTLEMEN.

Let it, then, when day is ended, etc.

FALK.

Wherefore seek the harvest's guerdon
  While the tree is yet in bloom?
Wherefore drudge beneath the burden
  Of an unaccomplished doom?
Wherefore let the scarecrow clatter
  Day and night upon the tree?
Brothers mine, the sparrows' chatter
  Has a cheerier melody.

CHORUS.

Brothers mine, the sparrow's chatter, etc.

FALK.

Happy songster! Wherefore scare him
  From our blossom-laden bower?
Rather for his music spare him
  All our future, flower by flower;
Trust me, 'twill be cheaply buying
  Present song with future fruit;
List the proverb, "Time is flying;—"
  Soon our garden music's mute.

CHORUS.

List the proverb, etc.

FALK.

I will live in song and gladness,—
  Then, when every bloom is shed,
Sweep together, scarce in sadness,
  All that glory, wan and dead:

Fling the gates wide! Bruise and batter,
Tear and trample, hoof and tusk;
I have plucked the flower, what matter
Who devours the withered husk!

CHORUS.

I have plucked the flower, etc.
[*They clink and empty their glasses.*

FALK (*to the ladies*).

There—that's the song you asked me for; but pray
Be lenient to it—I can't think to-day.

GULDSTAD.

Oh, never mind the sense—the sound's the thing.

MISS JAY (*looking round*).

But Svanhild, who was eagerest to hear—?
When Falk began, she suddenly took wing
And vanished—

ANNA (*pointing towards the back*).

No, for there she sits—I see her.

MRS HALM (*sighing*).

That child! Heaven knows, she's past my comprehending!

MISS JAY.

But, Mr Falk, I thought the lyric's ending
Was not so rich in—well, in poetry,
As others of the stanzas seemed to be.

STIVER.

Why yes, and I am sure it could not tax
Your powers to get a little more inserted—

FALK (*clinking glasses with him*).

You cram it in, like putty into cracks.
Till lean is into streaky fat converted.

STIVER (*unruffled*).

Yes, nothing easier—I, too, in my day
Could do the trick.

GULDSTAD.

Dear me! Were you a poet?

MISS JAY.

My Stiver! Yes!

STIVER.

Oh, in a humble way.

MISS JAY (*to the ladies*).

His nature is romantic.

MRS HALM.

Yes, we know it.

STIVER.

Not now; it's ages since I turned a rhyme.

FALK.

Yes, varnish and romance go off with time.
But in the old days —?

STIVER.

Well, you see, 'twas when
I was in love.

FALK.

Is that time over, then?
Have you slept off the sweet intoxication?

STIVER.

I'm now *engaged*—I hold official station—
That's better than *in love*, I apprehend!

FALK.

Quite so! You're in the right, my good old friend.
The worst is past—*vous voilà bien avancé*—
Promoted from mere lover to *fiancé*.

STIVER (*with a smile of complacent recollection*).

It's strange to think of it—upon my word,
I half suspect my memory of lying—

[*Turns to Falk.*

But seven years ago—it sounds absurd!—
I wasted office hours in versifying.

FALK.

What! Office hours—!

STIVER.

Yes, such were my transgressions.

GULDSTAD (*ringing on his glass*).

Silence for our solicitor's confessions!

STIVER.

But chiefly after five, when I was free,
I'd rattle off whole reams of poetry—
Ten—fifteen folios ere I went to bed—

FALK.

I see—you gave your Pegasus his head,
And off he tore—

STIVER.

On stamped or unstamped paper—
'Twas all the same to him—he'd prance and caper—

FALK.

The spring of poetry flowed no less flush?
But how, pray, did you teach it first to gush?

STIVER.

By aid of love's divining-rod, my friend!
Miss Jay it was that taught me where to bore,
My *fiancée*—she became so in the end—
For then she was—

FALK.

Your love and nothing more.

STIVER (*continuing*).

'Twas a strange time; I could not read a bit;
I tuned my pen instead of pointing it;
And when along the foolscap sheet it raced,
It twangled music to the words I traced;—
At last by letter I declared my flame
To her—to her—

FALK.

Whose *fiancé* you became.

STIVER.

In course of post her answer came to hand—
The motion granted—judgment in my favour!

FALK.

And you felt bigger, as you wrote, and braver,
To find you'd brought your venture safe to land!

STIVER.

Of course.

FALK.

And then you bade the Muse farewell?

STIVER.

I've felt no lyric impulse, truth to tell,
From that day forth. My vein appeared to peter
Entirely out; and now, if I essay
To turn a verse or two for New Year's Day,
I make the veriest hash of rhyme and metre,
And—I've no notion what the cause can be—
It turns to law and not to poetry.

GULDSTAD (*clinks glasses with him*).

And, trust me, you're no whit the worse for that!

[*To Falk.*

You think the stream of life is flowing solely
To bear you to the goal you're aiming at—
But you may find yourself mistaken wholly.
As for your song, perhaps it's most poetic,

Perhaps it's not—on that point we won't quarrel—
But here I lodge a protest energetic,
Say what you will, against its wretched moral.
A masterly economy and new
To let the birds play havoc at their pleasure
Among your fruit-trees, fruitless now for you,
And suffer flocks and herds to trample through
Your garden, and lay waste its springtide treasure!
A pretty prospect, truly, for next year!

FALK.

Oh, next, next, next! The thought I loathe and fear
That these four letters timidly express—
It beggars millionaires in happiness!
If I could be the autocrat of speech
But for one hour, that hateful word I'd banish;
I'd send it packing out of mortal reach,
As B and G from Knudsen's Grammar vanish.

STIVER.

Why should the word of hope enrage you thus?

FALK.

Because it darkens God's fair earth for us.
"Next year," "next love," "next life,"—my soul is vext
To see this world in thraldom to "the next."
'Tis this dull forethought, bent on future prizes,
That millionaires in gladness pauperises.
Far as the eye can reach, it blurs the age;
All rapture of the moment it destroys;
No one dares taste in peace life's simplest joys
Until he's struggled on another stage—

And there arriving, can he there repose?
No—to a new "next" off he flies again;
On, on, unresting, to the grave he goes;
And God knows if there's any resting then.

MISS JAY.

Fie, Mr Falk, such sentiments are shocking.

ANNA (*pensively*).

Oh, I can understand the feeling quite;
I am sure at bottom Mr Falk is right.

MISS JAY (*perturbed*).

My Stiver mustn't listen to his mocking.
He's rather too eccentric even now.—
My dear, I want you.

STIVER (*occupied in cleaning his pipe*).

Presently, my dear.

GULDSTAD (*to Falk*).

One thing at least to me is very clear;—
And that is that you cannot but allow
Some forethought indispensable. For see,
Suppose that you to-day should write a sonnet,
And, scorning forethought, you should lavish on it
Your last reserve, your all, of poetry,
So that, to-morrow, when you set about
Your next song, you should find yourself cleaned out,
Heavens! how your friends the critics then would crow!

FALK.

D'you think they'd notice I was bankrupt? No!
Once beggared of ideas, I and they
Would saunter arm in arm the self-same way—

[*Breaking off.*

But Lind! why, what's the matter with you, pray?
You sit there dumb and dreaming—I suspect you're
Deep in the mysteries of architecture.

LIND (*collecting himself*).

I? What should make you think so?

FALK.

I observe.
Your eyes are glued to the verandah yonder—
You're studying, mayhap, its arches' curve,
Or can it be its pillars' strength you ponder,
The door perhaps, with hammered iron hinges?
The window blinds, and their artistic fringes?
From something there your glances never wander.

LIND.

No, you are wrong—I'm just absorbed in being—
Drunk with the hour—naught craving, naught foreseeing.
I feel as though I stood, my life complete,
With all earth's riches scattered at my feet.
Thanks for your song of happiness and spring—
From out my inmost heart it seemed to spring.

[*Lifts his glass and exchanges a glance, unobserved, with Anna.*

Here's to the blossom in its fragrant pride!
What reck we of the fruit of autumn-tide?

[*Empties his glass.*

FALK (*looks at him with surprise and emotion, but assumes a light tone*).

Behold, fair ladies! though you scorn me quite,
Here I have made an easy proselyte.
His hymn-book yesterday was all he cared for—
To-day e'en dithyrambics he's prepared for!
We poets must be born, cries every judge;
But prose-folks, now and then, like Strasburg geese,
Gorge themselves so inhumanly obese
On rhyming balderdash and rhythmic fudge,
That, when cleaned out, their very souls are thick
With lyric lard and greasy rhetoric.

[*To Lind.*

Your praise, however, I shall not forget;
We'll sweep the lyre henceforward in duet.

MISS JAY.

You, Mr Falk, are hard at work, no doubt,
Here in these rural solitudes delightful,
Where at your own sweet will you roam about—

MRS HALM (*smiling*).

Oh no, his laziness is something frightful.

MISS JAY.

What! here at Mrs Halm's! that's most surprising—
Surely it's just the place for poetising—

[*Pointing to the right.*

That summer-house, for instance, in the wood
Sequestered, name me any place that could
Be more conducive to poetic mood—

FALK.

Let blindness veil the sunlight from mine eyes,
I'll chant the splendour of the sunlit skies!
Just for a season let me beg or borrow
A great, a crushing, a stupendous sorrow,
And soon you'll hear my hymns of gladness rise!
But best, Miss Jay, to nerve my wings for flight,
Find me a maid to be my life, my light—
For that incitement long to Heaven I've pleaded;
But hitherto, worse luck, it hasn't heeded.

MISS JAY.

What levity!

MRS HALM.

Yes, most irreverent!

FALK.

Pray don't imagine it was my intent
To live with her on bread and cheese and kisses.
No! just upon the threshold of our blisses,
Kind Heaven must snatch away the gift it lent.
I need a little spiritual gymnastic;
The dose in that form surely would be drastic.

SVANHILD

[*Has during the talk approached; she stands close to the table, and says in a determined but whimsical tone:*

I'll pray that such may be your destiny.
But, when it finds you—bear it like a man.

FALK (*turning round in surprise*).

Miss Svanhild!—well, I'll do the best I can.

But think you I may trust implicitly
To finding your petitions efficacious?
Heaven, as you know, to faith alone is gracious—
And though you've doubtless will enough for two
To make me bid my peace of mind adieu,
Have you the faith to carry matters through?
That is the question.

SVANHILD (*half in jest*).

Wait till sorrow comes,
And all your being's springtide chills and numbs,
Wait till it gnaws and rends you, soon and late,
Then tell me if my faith is adequate.

[*She goes across to the ladies.*

MRS HALM (*aside to her*).

Can you two never be at peace? you've made
Poor Mr Falk quite angry I'm afraid.

[*Continues reprovingly in a low voice. Miss Jay joins in the conversation. Svanhild remains cold and silent.*

FALK (*after a pause of reflection goes over to the summer-house, then to himself*).

With fullest confidence her glances lightened.
Shall I believe, as she does so securely,
That Heaven intends—

GULDSTAD.

No, hang it! don't be frightened!
The powers above would be demented surely
To give effect to orders such as these.

No, my good sir—the cure for your disease
Is exercise for muscle, nerve and sinew.
Don't lie there wasting all the grit that's in you
In idle dreams; cut wood, if that were all;
And then I'll say the devil's in't indeed
If one brief fortnight does not find you freed
From all your whimsies high-fantastical.

FALK.

Fetter'd by choice, like Burnell's ass, I ponder—
The flesh on this side, and the spirit yonder.
Which were it wiser I should go for first?

GULDSTAD (*filling the glasses*).

First have some punch—that quenches ire and thirst.

MISS HALM (*looking at her watch*).

Ha! Eight o'clock! my watch is either fast, or
It's just the time we may expect the Pastor.
[*Rises, and puts things in order on the verandah.*

FALK.

What! have we parsons coming?

MISS JAY.

Don't you know?

MRS HALM.

I told you, just a little while ago—

ANNA.

No, mother—Mr Falk had not yet come.

MRS HALM.

Why no, that's true; but pray don't look so glum.
Trust me, you'll be enchanted with his visit.

FALK.

A clerical enchanter; pray who is it?

MRS HALM.

Why, Pastor Strawman, not unknown to fame.

FALK.

Indeed! Oh yes, I think I've heard his name,
And read that in the legislative game
He comes to take a hand, with voice and vote.

STIVER.

He speaks superbly.

GULDSTAD.

When he's cleared his throat.

MISS JAY.

He's coming with his wife—

MRS HALM.

And all their blessings—

FALK.

To give them three or four days' treat, poor dears—
For soon he'll be immersed above the ears
In Swedish muddles and official messings—
I see!

MRS HALM (*to Falk*).

Now there's a man for you, in truth!

GULDSTAD.

They say he was a rogue, though, in his youth.

MISS JAY (*offended*).

There, Mr Gulstad, I must break a lance!
I've heard as long as I can recollect,
Most worthy people speak with great respect
Of Pastor Strawman and his life's romance.

GULDSTAD (*laughing*).

Romance?

MISS JAY.

Romance! I call a match romantic
At which mere worldly wisdom looks askance.

FALK.

You make my curiosity gigantic.

MISS JAY (*continuing*).

But certain people always grow splenetic—
Why, goodness knows—at everything pathetic,
And scoff it down. We all know how, of late,
An unfledged, upstart, undergraduate
Presumed with brazen insolence, to declare
That "William Russell" was a poor affair!

FALK.

But what has this to do with Strawman, pray?
Is he a poem, or a Christian play?

MISS JAY (*with tears of emotion*).

No, Falk,—a man, with heart as large as day.
But when a—so to speak—mere lifeless thing
Can put such venom into envy's sting,

And stir up evil passions fierce and fell
Of such a depth—

FALK (*sympathetically*).

And such a length as well—

MISS JAY.

Why then, a man of your commanding brain
Can't fail to see—

FALK.

Oh yes, that's very plain.
But hitherto I haven't quite made out
The nature, style, and plot of this romance.
It's something quite delightful I've no doubt—
But just a little inkling in advance—

STIVER.

I will abstract, in rapid *resumé*,
The leading points.

MISS JAY.

No, I am more *au fait*,
I know the ins and outs—

MRS HALM.

I know them too!

MISS JAY.

Oh Mrs Halm! now let me tell it, do!
Well, Mr Falk, you see—he passed at college
For quite a miracle of wit and knowledge,
Had admirable taste in books and dress—

MRS HALM.

And acted—privately—with great success.

MISS JAY.

Yes, wait a bit—he painted, played and wrote—

MRS HALM.

And don't forget his gift of anecdote.

MISS JAY.

Do give me time; I know the whole affair:
He made some verses, set them to an air,
Also his own,—and found a publisher.
O heavens! with what romantic melancholy
He played and sang his "Madrigals to Molly"!

MRS HALM.

He was a genius, that's the simple fact.

GULDSTAD (*to himself*).

Hm! Some were of opinion he was cracked.

FALK.

A gray old stager, whose sagacious head
Was never upon mouldy parchments fed,
Says "Love makes Petrarchs, just as many lambs
And little occupation, Abrahams."
But who was Molly?

MISS JAY.

Molly? His elect,
His lady-love, whom shortly we expect.
Of a great firm her father was a member—

GULDSTAD.

A timber house.

MISS JAY (*curtly*).

I'm really not aware.

GULDSTAD.

Did a large trade in scantlings, I remember.

MISS JAY.

That is the trivial side of the affair.

FALK.

A firm?

MISS JAY (*continuing*).

Of vast resources, I'm informed.
You can imagine how the suitors swarm'd;
Gentlemen of the highest reputation.—

MRS HALM.

Even a baronet made application.

MISS JAY.

But Molly was not to be made their catch.
She had met Strawman upon private stages;
To see him was to love him—

FALK.

And despatch
The wooing gentry home without their wages?

MRS HALM.

Was it not just a too romantic match?

MISS JAY.

And then there was a terrible old father,
Whose sport was thrusting happy souls apart;
She had a guardian also, as I gather,
To add fresh torment to her tortured heart.
But each of them was loyal to his vow;
A straw-thatched cottage and a snow-white ewe
They dream'd of, just enough to nourish two—

MRS HALM.

Or at the very uttermost a cow,—

MISS JAY.

In short, I've heard it from the lips of both,—
A beck, a byre, two bosoms, and one troth.

FALK.

Ah yes! And then—?

MISS JAY.

She broke with kin and class.

FALK.

She broke—?

MRS HALM.

Broke with them.

FALK.

There's a plucky lass!

MISS JAY.

And fled to Strawman's garret—

FALK.

How? Without—
Ahem—the priestly consecration?

MISS JAY.

Shame!

MRS HALM.

Fy, fy! my late beloved husband's name
Was on the list of sponsors—!

STIVER (*to Miss Jay*).

You're to blame
For leaving that important item out.
In a report 'tis of the utmost weight
That the chronology be accurate.
But what I never yet could comprehend
Is how on earth they managed—

FALK.

The one room
Not housing sheep and cattle, I presume.

MISS JAY (*to Stiver*).

O, but you must consider this, my friend;
There is no *Want* where Love's the guiding star;
All's right without if tender Troth's within.

[*To Falk.*

He loved her to the notes of the guitar,
And she gave lessons on the violin—

MRS HALM.

Then all, of course, on credit they bespoke—

GULDSTAD.

Till, in a year, the timber merchant broke.

MRS HALM.

Then Strawman had a call to north.

MISS JAY.

And there
Vowed, in a letter that I saw (as few did),
He lived but for his duty, and for her.

FALK (*as if completing her statement*).

And with those words his Life's Romance concluded.

MRS HALM (*rising*).

How if we should go out upon the lawn,
And see if there's no prospect of them yet?

MISS JAY (*drawing on her mantle*).

It's cool already.

MRS HALM.

Svanhild, will you get
My woollen shawl?—Come ladies, pray!

LIND (*to Anna, unobserved by the others*).

Go on!

[*Svanhild goes into the house; the others, except Falk, go towards the back and out to the left. Lind, who has followed, stops and returns.*

LIND.

My friend!

FALK.

Ah, ditto.

LIND.

Falk, your hand! The tide
Of joy's so vehement, it will perforce
Break out—

FALK.

Hullo there; you must first be tried;
Sentence and hanging follow in due course.
Now, what on earth's the matter? To conceal
From me, your friend, this treasure of your finding;
For you'll confess the inference is binding:
You've come into a prize off Fortune's wheel!

LIND.

I've snared and taken Fortune's blessed bird!

FALK.

How? Living,—and undamaged by the steel?

LIND.

Patience; I'll tell the matter in one word.
I am engaged! Conceive—!

FALK (*quickly*).

Engaged!

LIND.

It's true
To-day,—with unimagined courage swelling,
I said,—ahem, it will not bear re-telling;—

But only think,—the sweet young maiden grew
Quite rosy-red,—but not at all enraged!
You see, Falk, what I ventured for a bride!
She listened,—and I rather think she cried;
That, sure, means "Yes"?

FALK.

If precedents decide;
Go on.

LIND.

And so we really are—engaged?

FALK.

I should conclude so; but the only way
To be quite certain, is to ask Miss Jay.

LIND.

O no, I feel so confident, so clear!
So perfectly assured, and void of fear.
[*Radiantly in a mysterious tone.*
Hark! I had leave her fingers to caress
When from the coffee-board she drew the cover.

FALK (*lifting and emptying his glass*).

Well, flowers of spring your wedding garland dress!

LIND (*doing the same*).

And here I swear by heaven that I will love her
Until I die, with love as infinite
As now glows in me,—for she is so sweet!

FALK.

Engaged! Aha, so that was why you flung
The Holy Law and Prophets on the shelf!

LIND (*laughing*).

And you believed it was the song you sung—!

FALK.

A poet believes all things of himself.

LIND (*seriously*).

Don't think, however, Falk, that I dismiss
The theologian from my hour of bliss.
Only, I find the Book will not suffice
As Jacob's ladder unto Paradise.
I must into God's world, and seek Him there.
A boundless kindness in my heart upsprings,
I love the straw, I love the creeping things;
They also in my joy shall have a share.

FALK.

Yes, only tell me this, though—

LIND.

I have told it,—
My precious secret, and our three hearts hold it!

FALK.

But have you thought about the future?

LIND.

Thought?
I?—thought about the future? No, from this
Time forth I live but in the hour that is.
In home shall all my happiness be sought;
We hold Fate's reins, we drive her hither, thither,

And neither friend nor mother shall have right
To say unto my budding blossom: Wither!
For I am earnest and her eyes are bright,
And so it must unfold into the light!

FALK.

Yes, Fortune likes you, you will serve her turn!

LIND.

My spirits like wild music glow and burn;
I feel myself a Titan: though a foss
Opened before me—I would leap across!

FALK.

Your love, you mean to say, in simple prose,
Has made a reindeer of you.

LIND.

Well, suppose;
But in my wildest flight, I know the nest
In which my heart's dove longs to be at rest!

FALK

Well then, to-morrow it may fly *con brio*;
You're off into the hills with the quartette.
I'll guarantee you against cold and wet—

LIND.

Pooh, the quartette may go and climb in *trio*,
The lowly dale has mountain air for me;
Here I've the immeasurable fjord, the flowers,
Here I have warbling birds and choral bowers,
And lady Fortune's self,—for here is *she!*

FALK.

Ah, lady Fortune by our Northern water
Is *rara avis*,—hold her if you've caught her!
[*With a glance towards the house.*
Hist—Svanhild—

LIND.

Well ; I go,—disclose to none
The secret that we share alone with *one*.
'Twas good of you to listen : now enfold it
Deep in your heart,—warm, glowing, as I told it.

[*He goes out in the background to the others. Falk looks after him a moment, and paces up and down in the garden, visibly striving to master his agitation. Presently Svanhild comes out with a shawl on her arm, and is going towards the back. Falk approaches and gazes at her fixedly. Svanhild stops.*

SVANHILD (*after a short pause*).

You gaze so at me?

FALK (*half to himself*).

Yes, 'tis *there*—the same ;
The shadow in her eyes' deep mirror sleeping,
The roguish elf about her lips a-peeping,
It *is* there.

SVANHILD.

What? You frighten me.

FALK.

Your name
Is Svanhild?

SVANHILD.

Yes, you know it very well.

FALK.

But do *you* know the name is laughable?
I beg you to discard it from to-night!

SVANHILD.

That is far beyond a daughter's right—

FALK (*laughing*).

Hm. "Svanhild!" "Svanhild!"

[*With sudden gravity.*

With your earliest breath
How came you by this prophecy of death?

SVANHILD.

Is it so grim?

FALK.

No, lovely as a song,
But for our age too great and stern and strong.
How can a modern demoiselle fill out
The ideal that heroic name expresses?
No, no, discard it with your outworn dresses.

SVANHILD.

You mean the mythical princess, no doubt—

FALK.

Who, guiltless, died beneath the horse's feet.

SVANHILD.

But now such acts are clearly obsolete.
No, no, I'll mount his saddle! There's my place!
How often have I dreamt, in pensive ease,
He bore me, buoyant, through the world apace,
His mane a flag of freedom in the breeze!

FALK.

Yes, the old tale. In "pensive ease" no mortal
Is stopped by thwarting bar or cullis'd portal;
Fearless we cleave the æther without bound;
In practice, tho', we shrewdly hug the ground;
For all love life and, having choice, will choose it;
And no man dares to leap where he may lose it.

SVANHILD.

Yes! show me but the end, I'll spurn the shore;
But let the end be worth the leaping for!
A Ballarat beyond the desert sands—
Else each will stay exactly where he stands.

FALK (*sarcastically*).

I grasp the case;—the due conditions fail.

SVANHILD (*eagerly*).

Exactly: what's the use of spreading sail
When there is not a breath of wind astir?

FALK (*ironically*).

Yes, what's the use of plying whip and spur
When there is not a penny of reward
For him who tears him from the festal board,

And mounts, and dashes headlong to perdition?
Such doing for the deed's sake asks a knight,
And knighthood's now an idle superstition.
That was your meaning, possibly?

SVANHILD.

Quite right.
Look at that fruit tree in the orchard close,—
No blossom on its barren branches blows.
You should have seen last year with what brave airs
It staggered underneath its world of pears.

FALK (*uncertain*).

No doubt, but what's the moral you impute?

SVANHILD (*with finesse*).

O, among other things, the bold unreason
Of modern Zacharies who seek for fruit.
If the tree blossom'd to excess last season,
You must not crave the blossoms back in this.

FALK.

I knew you'd find your footing in the ways
Of old Romance.

SVANHILD.

Yes, modern virtue is
Of quite another stamp. Who now arrays
Himself to battle for the truth? Who'll stake
His life and person fearless for truth's sake?
Where is the hero?

FALK (*looking keenly at her*).

Where is the Valkyria?

SVANHILD (*shaking her head*).

Valkyrias find no market in this land!
When the faith lately was assailed in Syria,
Did *you* go out with the crusader-band?
No, but on paper you were warm and willing,—
And sent the "Clerical Gazette" a shilling.

[*Pause. Falk is about to retort, but checks himself, and goes into the garden.*

SVANHILD.

[*After watching him a moment, approaches him and asks gently:*

Falk, are you angry?

FALK.

No, I only brood,—

SVANHILD (*with thoughtful sympathy*).

You seem to be two natures, still at feud,—
Unreconciled—

FALK.

I know it well.

SVANHILD (*impetuously*).

But why?

FALK (*losing self-control*).

Why, why? Because I hate to go about
With soul bared boldly to the vulgar eye,

As Jock and Jennie hang their passions out;
To wear my glowing heart upon my sleeve,
Like women in low dresses. You, alone,
Svanhild, you only,—you, I did believe,—
Well, it is past, *that* dream, for ever flown.—

[*She goes to the summer-house and looks out; he follows.*

You listen—?

SVANHILD.

To another voice, that sings.
Hark! every evening when the sun's at rest,
A little bird floats hither on beating wings,—
See there—it darted from its leafy nest—
And, do you know, it is my faith,—as oft
As God makes any songless soul, He sends
A little bird to be her friend of friends,
And sing for ever in her garden-croft.

FALK (*picking up a stone*).

Then must the owner and the bird be near,
Or its song's squandered on a stranger's ear.

SVANHILD.

Yes, that is true; but I've discovered mine.
Of speech and song I am denied the power,
But when it warbles in its leafy bower,
Poems flow in upon my brain like wine—
Ah, yes,—they fleet—they are not to be won—

[*Falk throws the stone. Svanhild screams.*

O God, you've hit it! Ah, what have you done!

[*She hurries out to the right and then quickly returns.*

O pity! pity!

FALK (*in passionate agitation*).

No,—but eye for eye,
Svanhild, and tooth for tooth. Now you'll attend
No further greetings from your garden-friend,
No guerdon from the land of melody.
That is my vengeance : as you slew, I slay.

SVANHILD.

I slew?

FALK.

You slew. Until this very day,
A clear-voiced song-bird warbled in my soul;
See,—now one passing bell for both may toll—
You've killed it!

SVANHILD.

Have I?

FALK.

Yes, for you have slain
My young, high-hearted, joyous exultation—
[*Contemptuously*.
By your betrothal!

SVANHILD.

How! But pray, explain—!

FALK.

O, it's in full accord with expectation;
He gets his licence, enters orders, speeds to
A post,—as missionary in the West—

SVANHILD (*in the same tone*).

A pretty penny, also, he succeeds to ;—
For it is Lind you speak of—?

FALK.

You know best
Of whom I speak.

SVANHILD (*with a subdued smile*).

As the bride's sister, true,
I cannot help—

FALK.

Great God! It is not you—?

SVANHILD.

Who win this overplus of bliss? Ah no!

FALK (*with almost childish joy*).

It is not you! O God be glorified!
What love, what mercy does He not bestow!
I shall not see you as another's bride ;—
'Twas but the fire of pain He bade me bear—
[*Tries to seize her hand.*
O hear me, Svanhild, hear me then—

SVANHILD (*pointing quickly to the background*).

See there!

[*She goes towards the house. At the same moment Mrs Halm, Anna, Miss Jay, Guldstad, Stiver, and Lind emerge from the background. During the previous scene the sun has set; it is now dark.*

MRS HALM (*to Svanhild*).

The Strawmans may be momently expected.
Where have you been?

MISS JAY (*after glancing at Falk*).

Your colour's very high.

SVANHILD.

A little face-ache; it will soon pass by.

MRS HALM.

And yet you walk at nightfall unprotected?
Arrange the room, and see that tea is ready;
Let everything be nice; I know the lady.

[*Svanhild goes in.*

STIVER (*to Falk*).

What is the colour of this parson's coat?

FALK.

I guess bread-taxers would not catch his vote.

STIVER.

How if one made allusion to the store
Of verses, yet unpublished, in my drawer?

FALK.

It might do something.

STIVER.

Would to heaven it might!
Our wedding's imminent; our purses light.
Courtship's a very serious affair.

FALK.

Just so: *"Qu' allais-tu faire dans cette galère?"*

STIVER.

Is courtship a "galère"?

FALK.

No, married lives;—
All servitude, captivity, and gyves.

STIVER (*seeing Miss Jay approach*).

You little know what wealth a man obtains
From woman's eloquence and woman's brains.

MISS JAY (*aside to Stiver*).

Will Guldstad give us credit, think you?

STIVER (*peevishly*).

I
Am not quite certain of it yet: I'll try.

[*They withdraw in conversation; Lind and Anna approach.*

LIND (*aside to Falk*).

I can't endure it longer; in post-haste
I must present her—

FALK.

You had best refrain,
And not initiate the eye profane
Into your mysteries—

LIND.

That would be a jest!—
From you, my fellow-boarder, and my mate,
To keep concealed my new-found happy state!
Nay, now, my head with Fortune's oil anointed—

FALK.

You think the occasion good to get it *curled?*
Well, my good friend, you won't be disappointed;
Go and announce your union to the world!

LIND.

Other reflections also weigh with me,
And one of more especial gravity;
Say that there lurked among our motley band
Some sneaking, sly, pretender to her hand;
Say, his attentions became undisguised,—
We should be disagreeably compromised.

FALK.

Yes, it is true; it had escaped my mind,
You for a higher office were designed,
Love as his young licentiate has retained you;
Shortly you'll get a permanent position;
But it would be defying all tradition
If at the present moment he ordained you.

LIND.

Yes if the merchant does not—

FALK.

What of him?

ANNA (*troubled*).

Oh, it is Lind's unreasonable whim.

LIND.

Hush; I've a deep foreboding that the man
Will rob me of my treasure, if he can.
The fellow, as we know, comes daily down,
Is rich, unmarried, takes you round the town;
In short, my own, regard it as we will,
There are a thousand things that bode us ill.

ANNA (*sighing*).

Oh, it's too bad; to-day was so delicious!

FALK (*sympathetically to Lind*).

Don't wreck your joy, unfoundedly suspicious,
Don't hoist your flag till time the truth disclose—

ANNA.

Great God! Miss Jay is looking; hush, be still!
[*She and Lind withdraw in different directions.*

FALK (*looking after Lind*).

So to the ruin of his youth he goes.

GULDSTAD

(*Who has meantime been conversing on the steps with Mrs Halm and Miss Jay, approaches Falk and slaps him on the shoulder*).

Well, brooding on a poem?

FALK.

No, a play.

GULDSTAD.

The deuce;—I never heard it was your line.

FALK.

O no, the author is a friend of mine,
And your acquaintance also, I daresay.
The knave's a dashing writer, never doubt.
Only imagine, in a single day
He's worked a perfect little Idyll out.

GULDSTAD (*slily*).

With happy ending, doubtless!

FALK.

You're aware,
No curtain falls but on a plighted pair.
Thus with the Trilogy's First Part we've reckoned;
But now the poet's labour-throes begin;
The Comedy of Troth-plight, Part the Second,
Thro' five insipid Acts he has to spin,
And of that staple, finally, compose
Part Third,—or Wedlock's Tragedy, in prose.

GULDSTAD (*smiling*).

The poet's vein is catching, it would seem.

FALK.

Really? How so, pray?

GULDSTAD.

Since I also pore
And ponder over a poetic scheme,—

[*Mysteriously.*

An actuality—and not a dream.

FALK.

And pray, who is the hero of your theme?

GULDSTAD.

I'll tell you that to-morrow—not before.

FALK.

It is yourself!

GULDSTAD.

You think me equal to it?

FALK.

I'm sure no other mortal man could do it.
But then the heroine? No city maid,
I'll swear, but of the country, breathing balm?

GULDSTAD (*lifting his finger*).

Ah,—that's the point, and must not be betrayed!—
[*Changing his tone.*
Pray tell me your opinion of Miss Halm.

FALK.

O you're best able to pronounce upon her;
My voice can neither credit nor dishonour,—
[*Smiling.*
But just take care no mischief-maker blot
This fine poetic scheme of which you talk.
Suppose I were so shameless as to balk
The meditated climax of the plot?

GULDSTAD (*good-naturedly*).

Well, I would cry "Amen," and change my plan.

FALK.

What!

GULDSTAD.

Why, you see, you are a letter'd man;
How monstrous were it if your skill'd design
Were ruined by a bungler's hand like mine?
[*Retires to the background.*

FALK (*in passing, to Lind*).

Yes, you were right; the merchant's really scheming
The ruin of your new-won happiness.

LIND (*aside to Anna*).

Now then you see, my doubting was not dreaming;
We'll go this very moment and confess.
[*They approach Mrs Halm, who is standing with Miss Jay by the house.*

GULDSTAD (*conversing with Stiver*).

'Tis a fine evening.

STIVER.

Very likely,—when
A man's disposed—

GULDSTAD (*facetiously*).

What, all not running smooth
In true love's course?

STIVER.

Not that exactly—

FALK (*coming up*).

Then
With your engagement?

STIVER.

That's about the truth.

FALK.

Hurrah! Your spendthrift pocket has a groat
Or two still left, it seems, of poetry.

STIVER (*stiffly*).

I cannot see what poetry has got
To do with my engagement, or with me.

FALK.

You are not meant to see; when lovers prove
What love is, all is over with their love.

GULDSTAD (*to Stiver*).

But if there's matter for adjustment, pray
Let's hear it.

STIVER.

I've been pondering all day
Whether the thing is proper to disclose,
But still the Ayes are balanced by the Noes.

FALK.

I'll right you in one sentence. Ever since
As plighted lover you were first installed,
You've felt yourself, if I may say so, galled—

STIVER.

And sometimes to the quick.

FALK.

You've had to wince
Beneath a crushing load of obligations
That you'd send packing, if good form permitted.
That's what's the matter.

STIVER.

Monstrous accusations!
My legal debts I've honestly acquitted;
But other bonds next month are falling due;
[*To Guldstad.*
When a man weds, you see, he gets a wife—

FALK (*triumphant*).

Now your youth's heaven once again is blue,
There rang an echo from your old song-life!
That's how it is: I read you thro' and thro';
Wings, wings were all you wanted,—and a knife!

STIVER.

A knife?

FALK.

Yes, Resolution's knife, to sever
Each captive bond, and set you free for ever,
To soar—

STIVER (*angrily*).

Nay, now you're insolent beyond
Endurance! Me to charge with violation

Of law,—me, me with plotting to abscond!
It's libellous, malicious defamation,
Insult and calumny—

FALK.

Are you insane?
What is all this about? Explain! Explain!

GULDSTAD (*laughingly to Stiver*).

Yes, clear your mind of all this balderdash!
What do you want?

STIVER (*pulling himself together*).

A trifling loan in cash.

FALK.

A loan!

STIVER (*hurriedly to Guldstad*).

That is, I mean to say, you know,
A voucher for a ten pound note, or so.

MISS JAY (*to Lind and Anna*).

I wish you joy! How lovely, how delicious!

GULDSTAD (*going up to the ladies*).

Pray what has happened?

[*To himself.*] This was unpropitious.

FALK (*throws his arms about Stiver's neck*).

Hurrah! the trumpet's dulcet notes proclaim
A brother born to you in Amor's name!

[*Drags him to the others.*

MISS JAY (*to the gentlemen*).

Think! Lind and Anna—think!—have plighted hearts,
Affianced lovers!

MRS HALM (*with tears of emotion*).

'Tis the eighth in order
Who well-provided from this house departs;
[*To Falk.*
Seven nieces wedded—always with a boarder—
[*Is overcome; presses her handkerchief to her eyes.*

MISS JAY (*to Anna*).

Well, there will come a flood of gratulation!
[*Caresses her with emotion.*

LIND (*seizing Falk's hand*).

My friend, I walk in rapt intoxication!

FALK.

Hold! As a plighted man you are a member
Of Rapture's Temperance-association.
Observe its rules;—no orgies here, remember!
[*Turning to Guldstad sympathetically.*
Well, my good sir!

GULDSTAD (*beaming with pleasure*).

I think this promises
All happiness for both.

FALK (*staring at him*).

You seem to stand
The shock with exemplary self-command.
That's well.

GULDSTAD.

What do you mean, sir?

FALK.

Only this;
That inasmuch as you appeared to feed
Fond expectations of your own—

GULDSTAD.

Indeed?

FALK.

At any rate, you were upon the scent.
You named Miss Halm; you stood upon this spot
And asked me—

GULDSTAD (*smiling*).

There are two, though, are there not?

FALK.

It was—the other sister that you meant?

GULDSTAD.

That sister, yes, the other one,—just so.
Judge for yourself, when you have come to know
That sister better, if she has not in her
Merits which, if they were divined, would win her
A little more regard than we bestow.

FALK (*coldly*).

Her virtues are of every known variety,
I'm sure.

GULDSTAD.

Not quite ; the accent of society
She cannot hit exactly ; there she loses.

FALK.

A grievous fault.

GULDSTAD.

But if her mother chooses
To spend a winter on her, she'll come out of it
Queen of them all, I'll wager.

FALK.

Not a doubt of it.

GULDSTAD (*laughing*).

Young women are odd creatures, to be sure !

FALK (*gaily*).

Like winter rye-seed, canopied secure
By frost and snow, invisibly they sprout.

GULDSTAD.

Then in the festive ball-room bedded out—

FALK.

With equivoque and scandal for manure—

GULDSTAD.

And when the April sun shines—

FALK.

There the blade is ;
The seed shot up in minnikin green ladies !
[*Lind comes up and seizes Falk's hand.*

LIND.

How well I chose,—past understanding well ;—
I feel a bliss that nothing can dispel.

GULDSTAD.

There stands your mistress ; tell us, if you can,
The right demeanour for a plighted man.

LIND (*perturbed*).

That's a third person's business to declare.

GULDSTAD (*joking*).

Ill-tempered ! This to Anna's ears I'll bear.
[*Goes to the ladies.*

LIND (*looking after him*).

Can such a man be tolerated ?

FALK.

You
Mistook his aim, however,—

LIND.

And how so ?

FALK.

It was not Anna that he had in view.

LIND.

How, was it Svanhild?

FALK.

Well, I hardly know.

[*Whimsically.*

Forgive me, martyr to another's cause!

LIND.

What do you mean?

FALK.

You've read the news to-night?

LIND.

No.

FALK.

Do so. There 'tis told in black and white
Of one who, ill-luck's bitter counsel taking,
Had his sound teeth extracted from his jaws
Because his cousin-german's teeth were aching.

MISS JAY (*looking out to the left*).

Here comes the priest!

MRS HALM.

Now see a man of might!

STIVER.

Five children, six, seven, eight—

FALK.

And, heavens, all recent!

MISS JAY.

Ugh! it is almost to be called indecent.

[*A carriage has meantime been heard stopping outside to the left. Strawman, his wife, and eight little girls, all in travelling dress, enter one by one.*

MRS HALM (*advancing to meet them*).

Welcome, a hearty welcome!

STRAWMAN.

Thank you.

MRS STRAWMAN.

Is it

A party?

MRS HALM.

No, dear madam, not at all.

MRS STRAWMAN.

If we disturb you—

MRS HALM.

Au contraire, your visit

Could in no wise more opportunely fall.

My Anna's just engaged.

STRAWMAN (*shaking Anna's hand with unction*).

Ah then, I must

Bear witness;—Lo! in wedded Love's presented

A treasure such as neither moth nor rust

Consumes—if it be duly supplemented.

MRS HALM.

But how delightful that your little maids
Should follow you to town.

STRAWMAN.

Four tender blades
We have besides.

MRS HALM.

Ah, really?

STRAWMAN.

Three of whom
Are still too infantine to take to heart
A loving father's absence, when I come
To town for sessions.

MISS JAY (*to Mrs Halm, bidding farewell*).

Now I must depart.

MRS HALM.

O, it is still so early!

MISS JAY.

I must fly
To town and spread the news. The Storms, I know,
Go late to rest, they will be up; and oh!
How glad the aunts will be! Now, dear, put by
Your shyness; for to-morrow a spring-tide
Of callers will flow in from every side!

MRS HALM.

Well, then, good-night.

[*To the others.*

Now friends, what would you say
To drinking tea?

[*To Mrs Strawman.*

Pray, madam, lead the way.

[*Mrs Halm, Strawman, his wife and children, with Guldstad, Lind, and Anna go into the house.*

MISS JAY (*taking Stiver's arm*).

Now let's be tender! Look how softly floats
Queen Luna on her throne o'er lawn and lea!
Well, but you are not looking!

STIVER (*crossly*).

Yes, I see;
I'm thinking of the promissory notes.

[*They go out to the left. Falk, who has been continuously watching Strawman and his wife, remains behind alone in the garden. It is now dark; the house is lighted up.*

FALK.

All is as if burnt out;—all desolate, dead—!
So thro' the world they wander, two and two;
Charred wreckage, like the blackened stems that strew
The forest when the withering fire is fled.
Far as the eye can travel, all is drought,
And nowhere peeps one spray of verdure out!

[*Svanhild comes out on to the verandah with a flowering rose-tree which she sets down.*

Yes one—yes one—!

SVANHILD.

Falk, in the dark?

FALK.

And fearless?
Darkness to me is fair, and light is cheerless.
But are not *you* afraid in yonder walls
Where the lamp's light on sallow corpses falls—

SVANHILD.

Shame!

FALK

(*Looking after Strawman who appears at the window*).

He was once so brilliant and so strong;
Warred with the world to win his mistress; passed
For Custom's doughtiest iconoclast;
And poured forth love in pæans of glad song—!
Look at him now! In solemn robes and wraps,
A two-legged drama on his own collapse!
And she, the limp-skirt slattern, with the shoes
Heel-trodden, that squeak and clatter in her traces,
This is the winged maid who was his Muse
And escort to the kingdom of the graces!
Of all that fire this puff of smoke's the end!
Sic transit gloria amoris, friend.

SVANHILD.

Yes, it is wretched, wretched past compare.
I know of no one's lot that I would share.

FALK (*eagerly*).

Then let us two rise up and bid defiance
To this same order Art, not Nature, bred!

SVANHILD (*shaking her head*).

Then were the cause for which we made alliance
Ruined, as sure as this is earth we tread.

FALK.

No, triumph waits upon two souls in unity.
To Custom's parish-church no more we'll wend,
Seatholders in the Philistine community.
See, Personality's one aim and end
Is to be independent, free and true.
In that I am not wanting, nor are you.
A fiery spirit pulses in your veins,
For thoughts that master, you have words that burn;
The corslet of convention, that constrains
The beating hearts of other maids, you spurn.
The voice that you were born with will not chime to
The chorus Custom's baton gives the time to.

SVANHILD.

And do you think pain has not often pressed
Tears from my eyes, and quiet from my breast?
I longed to shape my way to my own bent—

FALK.

"In pensive ease?"

SVANHILD.

O no, 'twas sternly meant.

But then the aunts came in with well-intended
Advice, the matter must be sifted, weighed—

[*Coming nearer.*

"In pensive ease," you say; oh no, I made
A bold experiment—in art.

FALK.

Which ended—?

SVANHILD.

In failure. I lacked talent for the brush.
The thirst for freedom, tho', I could not crush;
Checked at the easel, it essayed the stage—

FALK.

That plan was shattered also, I engage?

SVANHILD.

Upon the eldest aunt's suggestion, yes;
She much preferred a place as governess—

FALK.

But of all this I never heard a word!

SVANHILD (*smiling*).

No wonder; they took care that none was heard.
They trembled at the risk "my future" ran
If this were whispered to unmarried Man.

FALK (*after gazing a moment at her in meditative sympathy*).

That such must be your lot I long had guessed.
When first I met you, I can well recall,

You seemed to me quite other than the rest,
Beyond the comprehension of them all.
They sat at table,—fragrant tea a-brewing,
And small-talk humming with the tea in tune,
The young girls blushing and the young men cooing,
Like pigeons on a sultry afternoon.
Old maids and matrons volubly averred
Morality and faith's supreme felicity,
Young wives were loud in praise of domesticity,
While you stood lonely like a mateless bird.
And when at last the gabbling clamour rose
To a tea-orgy, a debauch of prose,
You seemed a piece of silver, newly minted,
Among foul notes and coppers dulled and dinted.
You were a coin imported, alien, strange,
Here valued at another rate of change,
Not passing current in that babel mart
Of poetry and butter, cheese and art.
Then—while Miss Jay in triumph took the field—

SVANHILD (*gravely*).

Her knight behind her, like a champion bold,
His hat upon his elbow, like a shield—

FALK.

Your mother nodded to your untouched cup:
"Drink, Svanhild dear, before your tea grows cold."
And then you drank the vapid liquor up,
The mawkish brew beloved of young and old.
But that name gripped me with a sudden spell;
The grim old Völsungs as they fought and fell,
With all their faded æons, seemed to rise

In never-ending line before my eyes.
In you I saw a Svanhild, like the old,
But fashioned to the modern age's mould.
Sick of its hollow warfare is the world;
Its lying banner it would fain have furled;
But when the world does evil, its offence
Is blotted in the blood of innocence.

SVANHILD (*with gentle irony*).

I think, at any rate, the fumes of tea
Must answer for that direful fantasy;
But 'tis your least achievement, past dispute,
To hear the spirit speaking, when 'tis mute.

FALK (*with emotion*).

Nay, Svanhild, do not jest: behind your scoff
Tears glitter,—O, I see them plain enough.
And I see more: when you to dust are fray'd,
And kneaded to a formless lump of clay,
Each bungling dilettante's scalpel-blade
On you his dull devices shall display.
The world usurps the creature of God's hand
And sets its image in the place of His,
Transforms, enlarges that part, lightens this;
And when upon the pedestal you stand
Complete, cries out in triumph: "*Now* she is
At last what woman ought to be: Behold,
How plastically calm, how marble-cold!
Bathed in the lamplight's soft irradiation,
How well in keeping with the decoration!"

[*Passionately seizing her hand.*

But if you are to die, live first! Come forth
With me into the glory of God's earth!
Soon, soon the gilded cage will claim its prize.
The Lady thrives there, but the Woman dies,
And I love nothing but the Woman in you.
There, if they will, let others woo and win you,
But here, my spring of life began to shoot,
Here my Song-tree put forth its firstling fruit;
Here I found wings and flight:—Svanhild, I know it,
Only be mine,—here I shall grow a poet!

SVANHILD (*in gentle reproof, withdrawing her hand*).

O, why have you betrayed yourself? How sweet
It was when we as friends could freely meet!
You should have kept your counsel. Can we stake
Our bliss upon a word that we may break?
Now you have spoken, all is over.

FALK.

No!
I've pointed to the goal,—now leap with me,
My high-souled Svanhild—if you dare, and show
That you have heart and courage to be free.

SVANHILD.

Be free?

FALK.

Yes, free, for freedom's all-in-all
Is absolutely to fulfil our Call.
And you by heaven were destined, I know well,
To be my bulwark against beauty's spell.

I, like my falcon namesake, have to swing
Against the wind, if I would reach the sky!
You are the breeze I must be breasted by,
You, only you, put vigour in my wing:
Be mine, be mine, until the world shall take you,
When leaves are falling, then our paths shall part.
Sing unto me the treasures of your heart,
And for each song another song I'll make you;
So may you pass into the lamplit glow
Of age, as forests fade without a throe.

SVANHILD (*with suppressed bitterness*).

I cannot thank you, for your words betray
The meaning of your kind solicitude.
You eye me as a boy a sallow, good
To cut and play the flute on for a day.

FALK.

Yes, better than to linger in the swamp
Till autumn choke it with her grey mists damp!

[*Vehemently*.

You must! you shall! To me you must present
What God to you so bountifully lent.
I speak in song what you in dreams have meant.
See yonder bird I innocently slew,
Her warbling was Song's book of books for you.
O, yield your music as she yielded hers!
My life shall be that music set to verse!

SVANHILD.

And when you know me, when my songs are flown,
And my last requiem chanted from the bough,—
What then?

FALK (*observing her*).

What then? Ah well, remember now!
[*Pointing to the garden.*

SVANHILD (*gently*).

Yes, I remember you can drive a stone.

FALK (*with a scornful laugh*).

This is your vaunted soul of freedom therefore!
All daring, if it had an end to dare for! [*Vehemently.*
I've shown you one; now, once for all, your yea
Or nay.

SVANHILD.

You know the answer I must make you:
I never can accept you in your way.

FALK (*coldly, breaking off*).

Then there's an end of it; the world may take you!
[*Svanhild has silently turned away. She supports her hands upon the verandah railing, and rests her head upon them.*

FALK

[*Walks several times up and down, takes a cigar, stops near her and says, after a pause:*

You think the topic of my talk to-night
Extremely ludicrous, I should not wonder?
[*Pauses for an answer. Svanhild is silent.*
I'm very conscious that it was a blunder;
Sister's and daughter's love alone possess you;

Henceforth I'll wear kid gloves when I address you,
Sure, so, of being understood aright.

[*Pauses, but as Svanhild remains motionless, he turns and goes towards the right.*

SVANHILD

(*Lifting her head after a brief silence, looking at him and drawing nearer*).

Now I will recompense your kind intent
To save me, with an earnest admonition.
That falcon-image gave me sudden vision
What your "emancipation" really meant.
You said you were the falcon, that must fight
Athwart the wind if it would reach the sky,
I was the breeze you must be breasted by,
Else vain were all your faculty of flight;
How pitifully mean! How paltry! Nay
How ludicrous, as you yourself divined!
That seed, however, fell not by the way,
But bred another fancy in my mind
Of a far more illuminating kind.
You, as I saw it, were no falcon, but
A tuneful dragon, out of paper cut,
Whose Ego holds a secondary station,
Dependent on the string for animation;
Its breast was scrawled with promises to pay
In cash poetic,—at some future day;
The wings were stiff with barbs and shafts of wit
That wildly beat the air, but never hit;
The tail was a satiric rod in pickle
To castigate the town's infirmities,
But all it compass'd was to lightly tickle

The casual doer of some small amiss.
So you lay helpless at my feet, imploring:
"O raise me, how and where is all the same!
Give me the power of singing and of soaring,
No matter at what cost of bitter blame!"

FALK (*clenching his fists in inward agitation*).

Heaven be my witness—!

SVANHILD.

No, you must be told:—
For such a childish sport I am too old.
But you, whom Nature made for high endeavour,
Are you content the fields of air to tread
Hanging your poet's life upon a thread
That at my pleasure I can slip and sever?

FALK (*hurriedly*).

What is the date to-day?

SVANHILD (*more gently*).

Why, now, that's right!
Mind well this day, and heed it, and beware;
Trust to your own wings only for your flight,
Sure, if they do not break, that they will bear.
The paper poem for the desk is fit,
That which is lived alone has life in it;
That only has the wings that scale the height;
Choose now between them, poet: be, or write!

[*Nearer to him.*

Now I have done what you besought me; now
My requiem is chanted from the bough;

My only one ; now all my songs are flown ;
Now, if you will, I'm ready for the stone !

[*She goes into the house ; Falk remains motionless, looking after her ; far out on the fjord is seen a boat, from which the following chorus is faintly heard :*

CHORUS.

My wings I open, my sail spread wide,
And cleave like an eagle life's glassy tide ;
  Gulls follow my furrow's foaming ;
Overboard with the ballast of care and cark ;
And what if I shatter my roaming bark,
  It is passing sweet to be roaming !

FALK (*starting from a reverie*).

What, music ? Ah, it will be Lind's quartette
Getting their jubilation up.—Well met !

[*To Guldstad, who enters with an overcoat on his arm.*

Ah, slipping off, sir ?

GULDSTAD.

Yes, with your goodwill.
But let me first put on my overcoat.
We prose-folks are susceptible to chill ;
The night wind takes us by the tuneless throat.
Good evening !

FALK.

Sir, a word ere you proceed !
Show me a task, a mighty one, you know— !
I'm going in for life— !

GULDSTAD (*with ironical emphasis*).

Well, in you go!
You'll find that you are *in* for it, indeed.

FALK (*looking reflectively at him, says slowly*).

There is my program, furnished in a phrase.
[*In a lively outburst.*
Now I have wakened from my dreaming days,
I've cast the die of life's supreme transaction,
I'll show you—else the devil take me—

GULDSTAD.

Fie,
No cursing: curses never scared a fly.

FALK.

Words, words, no more, but action, only action!
I will reverse the plan of the Creation;—
Six days were lavish'd in that occupation;
My world's still lying void and desolate,
Hurrah, to-morrow, Sunday—I'll create!

GULDSTAD (*laughing*).

Yes, strip, and tackle it like a man, that's right!
But first go in and sleep on it. Good-night!

[*Goes out to the left. Svanhild appears in the room over the verandah; she shuts the window and draws down the blind.*

FALK.

No, first I'll act. I've slept too long and late.

[*Looks up at Svanhild's window, and exclaims, as if seized with a sudden resolution:*

Good-night! Good-night! Sweet dreams to-night be thine;
To-morrow, Svanhild, thou art plighted mine!

[*Goes out quickly to the right; from the water the Chorus is heard again.*

CHORUS.

Maybe I shall shatter my roaming bark,
But it's passing sweet to be roaming!

[*The boat slowly glides away as the curtain falls.*

ACT II.

Sunday afternoon. Well-dressed ladies and gentlemen are drinking coffee on the verandah. Several of the guests appear through the open glass door in the garden-room: the following song is heard from within.

CHORUS.

Welcome, welcome, new plighted pair
To the merry ranks of the plighted!
Now you may revel as free as air,
Caress without stint and kiss without care,—
No longer of footfall affrighted.

Now you are licensed, wherever you go,
To the rapture of cooing and billing;
Now you have leisure love's seed to sow,
Water, and tend it, and make it grow;—
Let us see you've a talent for tilling!

MISS JAY (*within*).

Ah Lind, if only I had chanced to hear,
I would have teased you!

A Lady (*within*).

How vexatious though!

Another Lady (*in the doorway*).

Dear Anna, did he ask in *writing?*

An Aunt.

No!

Miss Jay.

Mine did.

A Lady (*on the verandah*).

How long has it been secret, dear?

[*Runs into the room.*

Miss Jay.

To-morrow there will be the ring to choose.

Ladies (*eagerly*).

We'll take his measure!

Miss Jay.

Nay; that *she* must do.

Mrs Strawman

(*on the verandah, to a lady who is busy with embroidery*).

What kind of knitting-needles do you use?

A Servant (*in the door with a coffee-pot*).

More coffee, madam?

A Lady.

Thanks, a drop or two.

MISS JAY (*to Anna*).

How fortunate you've got your new manteau
Next week to go your round of visits in!

AN ELDERLY LADY (*at the window*).

When shall we go and order the trousseau?

MRS STRAWMAN.

How are they selling cotton-bombasine?

A GENTLEMAN (*to some ladies on the verandah*).

Just look at Lind and Anna; what's his sport?

LADIES (*with shrill ecstacy*).

Gracious, he kissed her glove!

OTHERS (*similarly, springing up*).

No! Kiss'd it? Really?

LIND (*appears, red and embarrassed, in the doorway*).

O, stuff and nonsense!

[*Disappears.*

MISS JAY.

Yes, I saw it clearly.

STIVER
(*in the door, with a coffee-cup in one hand and a biscuit in the other*).

The witnesses must not mislead the court;
I here make affidavit, they're in error.

MISS JAY (*within*).

Come forward, Anna; stand before this mirror!

SOME LADIES (*calling*).

You too, Lind!

MISS JAY.

Back to back! A little nearer!

LADIES.

Come, let us see by how much she is short.

[*All run into the garden-room; laughter and shrill talk are heard for a while from within.*

[*Falk, who during the preceding scene has been walking about in the garden, advances into the foreground, stops and looks in until the noise has somewhat abated.*

FALK.

There love's romance is being done to death.—
The butcher once who boggled at the slaughter,
Prolonging needlessly the ox's breath,—
He got his twenty days of bread and water;
But these—these butchers yonder—they go free.
[*Clenches his fist.*
I could be tempted—; hold, words have no worth,
I've sworn it, action only from henceforth!

LIND (*coming hastily but cautiously out*).

Thank God, they're talking fashions; now's my chance
To slip away—

FALK.

Ha, Lind, *you've* drawn the prize
Of luck,—congratulations buzz and dance
All day about you, like a swarm of flies.

LIND.

They're all at heart so kindly and so nice;
But rather fewer clients would suffice.
Their helping hands begin to gall and fret me;
I'll get a moment's respite, if they'll let me.
[*Going out to the right.*

FALK.

Whither away?

LIND.

Our den;—it has a lock;
In case you find the oak is sported, knock.

FALK.

But shall I not fetch Anna to you?

LIND.

No—
If she wants anything, she'll let me know.
Last night we were discussing until late;
We've settled almost everything of weight;
Besides I think it scarcely goes with piety
To have too much of one's beloved's society.

FALK.

Yes, you are right; for daily food we need
A simple diet.

LIND.

Pray excuse me, friend.
I want a whiff of reason and the weed ;
I haven't smoked for three whole days on end.
My blood was pulsing in such agitation,
I trembled for rejection all the time—

FALK.

Yes, you may well desire recuperation—

LIND.

And won't tobacco's flavour be sublime !

[*Goes out to the right. Miss Jay and some other Ladies come out of the garden-room.*

MISS JAY (*to Falk*).

That was *he* surely ?

FALK.

Yes, your hunted deer.

LADIES.

To run away from us !

OTHERS.

For shame ! For shame

FALK.

'Tis a bit shy at present, but, no fear,
A week of servitude will make him tame.

MISS JAY (*looking round*).

Where is he hid ?

FALK.

His present hiding-place
Is in the garden loft, our common lair; [*Blandly.*
But let me beg you not to seek him there;
Give him a breathing time!

MISS JAY.

Well, good: the grace
Will not be long, tho'.

FALK.

Nay, be generous!
Ten minutes,—then begin the game again.
He has an English sermon on the brain.

MISS JAY.

An English—?

LADIES.

O you laugh! You're fooling us!

FALK.

I'm in grim earnest. 'Tis his fixed intention
To take a charge among the emigrants,
And therefore—

MISS JAY (*with horror*).

Heavens, he had the face to mention
That mad idea? [*To the ladies.*
O quick—fetch all the aunts!
Anna, her mother, Mrs Strawman too.

LADIES (*agitated*).

This must be stopped!

ALL.

We'll make a great ado!

MISS JAY.

Thank God, they're coming.

[*To Anna, who comes from the garden-room with Strawman, his wife and children, Stiver, Guldstad, Mrs Halm and the other guests.*

MISS JAY.

Do you know what Lind
Has secretly determined in his mind?
To go as missionary—

ANNA.

Yes, I know.

MRS HALM.

And you've agreed—!

ANNA (*embarrassed*).

That I will also go.

MISS JAY (*indignant*).

He's talked this stuff to you!

LADIES (*clasping their hands together*).

What tyranny!

FALK.

But think, his Call that would not be denied—!

MISS JAY.

Tut, that's what people follow when they're free:
A bridegroom follows nothing but his bride.—
No, my sweet Anna, ponder, I entreat:
You, reared in comfort from your earliest breath—?

FALK.

Yet, sure, to suffer for the faith is sweet!

MISS JAY.

Is one to suffer for one's bridegroom's faith?
That is a rather novel point of view.

[*To the ladies.*

Ladies, attend!

[*Takes Anna's arm.*

Now listen; then repeat
For his instruction what he has to do.

[*They go into the background and out to the right in eager talk with several of the ladies; the other guests disperse in groups about the garden. Falk stops Strawman, whose wife and children keep close to him. Guldstad goes to and fro during the following conversation.*

FALK.

Come, pastor, help young fervour in its fight,
Before they lure Miss Anna from her vows.

STRAWMAN (*in clerical cadence*).

The wife must be submissive to the spouse;—

[*Reflecting*

But if I apprehended him aright,

His Call's a problematical affair,
The Offering altogether in the air—

FALK.

Pray do not judge so rashly. I can give
You absolute assurance, as I live,
His Call is definite and incontestable—

STRAWMAN (*seeing it in a new light*).

Ah—if there's something fixed—investable—
Per annum—then I've nothing more to say.

FALK (*impatiently*).

You think the most of what I count the least ;
I mean the *inspiration,*—not the *pay* !

STRAWMAN (*with an unctuous smile*).

Pay is the first condition of a priest
In Asia, Africa, America,
Or where you will. Ah yes, if he were free,
My dear young friend, I willingly agree,
The thing might pass ; but, being pledged and bound,
He'll scarcely find the venture very sound.
Reflect, he's young and vigorous, sure to found
A little family in time ; assume his will
To be the very best on earth—but still
The *means,* my friend—? 'Build not upon the sand,'
Says Scripture. If, upon the other hand,
The Offering—

FALK.

That's no trifle, I'm aware.

STRAWMAN.

Ah, come—that wholly alters the affair.
When men are zealous in their Offering,
And liberal—

FALK.

There he far surpasses most.

STRAWMAN.

"He" say you? How? In virtue of his post
The Offering is not what he has to *bring*
But what he has to *get*.

MRS STRAWMAN (*looking towards the background*).

They're sitting there.

FALK (*after staring a moment in amazement, suddenly understands and bursts out laughing*).

Hurrah for Offerings—the ones that caper
And strut—on Holy-days—in bulging paper!

STRAWMAN.

All the year round the curb and bit we bear,
But Whitsuntide and Christmas make things square.

FALK (*gaily*).

Why then, provided only there's enough of it,
Even family-founders will obey their Calls.

STRAWMAN.

Of course; a man assured the *quantum suff.* of it
Will preach the Gospel to the cannibals.

[*Sotto voce.*

Now I must see if she cannot be led,

[*To one of the little girls.*

My little Mattie, fetch me out my head—
My pipe-head I should say, my little dear—

[*Feels in his coat-tail pocket.*

Nay, wait a moment tho': I have it here.

[*Goes across and fills his pipe, followed by his wife and children.*

GULDSTAD (*approaching*).

You seem to play the part of serpent in
This paradise of lovers.

FALK.

O, the pips
Upon the tree of knowledge are too green
To be a lure for anybody's lips.

[*To Lind, who comes in from the right.*

Ha, Lind!

LIND.

In heaven's name, who's been ravaging
Our sanctum? There the lamp lies dashed
To pieces, curtain dragged to floor, pen smashed,
And on the mantelpiece the inkpot splashed—

FALK (*clapping him on the shoulder*).

This wreck's the first announcement of my spring;
No more behind drawn curtains I will sit,
Making pen poetry with lamp alit;
My dull domestic poetising's done,
I'll walk by day, and glory in the sun:
My spring is come, my soul has broken free,
Action henceforth shall be my poetry.

LIND.

Make poetry of what you please for me;
But how if Mrs Halm should take amiss
Your breaking of her furniture to pieces?

FALK.

What!—she, who lays her daughters and her nieces
Upon the altar of her boarders' bliss,—
She frown at such a bagatelle as this!

LIND (*angrily*).

It's utterly outrageous and unfair,
And compromises me as well as you!
But that's her business, settle it with her.
The lamp was mine, tho', shade and burner too—

FALK.

Tut, on that head, I've no account to render;
You have God's summer sunshine in its splendour,—
What would you with the lamp?

LIND.

You are grotesque;
You utterly forget that summer passes;
If I'm to make a figure in my classes
At Christmas I must buckle to my desk.

FALK (*staring at him*).

What, you look *forward*?

LIND.

To be sure I do,
The examination's amply worth it too.

FALK.

Ah but—you 'only sit and live'—remember!
Drunk with the moment, you demand no more—
Not even a modest third-class next December.
You've caught the bird of Fortune fair and fleet,
You feel as if the world with all its store
Were scattered in profusion at your feet.

LIND.

Those were my words; they must be understood,
Of course, *cum grano salis*—

FALK.

Very good!

LIND.

In the *forenoons* I will enjoy my bliss;
That I am quite resolved on—

FALK.

Daring man!

LIND.

I have my round of visits to the clan;
Time will run anyhow to waste in this;
But any further dislocation of
My study-plan I strongly disapprove.

FALK.

A week ago, however, you were bent
On going out into God's world with song.

LIND.

Yes, but I thought the tour a little long;
The fourteen days might well be better spent.

FALK.

Nay, but you had another argument
For staying; how the lovely dale for you
Was mountain air and winged warble too.

LIND.

Yes, to be sure, this air is unalloyed;
But all its benefits may be enjoyed
Over one's book without the slightest bar.

FALK.

But it was just *the Book* which failed, you see,
As Jacob's ladder—

LIND.

How perverse you are!
That is what people say when they are *free*—

FALK.

(*Looking at him and folding his hands in silent amazement*).

Thou also, Brutus!

LIND (*with a shade of confusion and annoyance*).

Pray remember, do!
That I have other duties now than you;
I have my fiancée. Every plighted pair,
Those of prolonged experience not excepted,—
Whose evidence you would not wish rejected,—

Will tell you, that if two are bound to fare
Through life together, they must—

FALK.

Prithee spare
The comment; who supplied it?

LIND.

Well, we'll say
Stiver, he's honest surely; and Miss Jay,
Who has such very great experience here,
She says—

FALK.

Well, but the Parson and his dear?

LIND.

Yes, they're remarkable. There broods above
Them such placidity, such quietude,—
Conceive, she can't remember being wooed,
Has quite forgotten what is meant by love.

FALK.

Ah, yes, when one has slumber'd over long,
The birds of memory refuse their song.
[*Laying his hand on Lind's shoulder, with an ironical look.*
You, Lind, slept sound last night, I guarantee?

LIND.

And long. I went to bed in such depression,
And yet with such a fever in my brain,
I almost doubted if I could be sane.

FALK.

Ah yes, a sort of witchery, you see.

LIND.

Thank God I woke in perfect self-possession.

[*During the foregoing scene Strawman has been seen from time to time walking in the background in lively conversation with Anna; Mrs Strawman and the children follow. Miss Jay now appears also, and with her Mrs Halm and other ladies.*

MISS JAY (*before she enters*).

Ah, Mr Lind.

LIND (*to Falk*).

They're after me again!
Come, let us go.

MISS JAY.

Nay, nay, you must remain,
Let us make speedy end of the division
That has crept in between your love and you.

LIND.

Are we divided?

MISS JAY (*pointing to Anna, who is standing further off in the garden*).

Gather the decision
From yon red eyes. The foreign mission drew
Those tears.

LIND.

But heavens, she was glad to go—

MISS JAY (*scoffing*).

Yes, to be sure, one would imagine so!
No, my dear Lind, you'll take another view
When you have heard the whole affair discussed;

LIND.

But then this warfare for the faith, you know,
Is my most cherished dream!

MISS JAY.

O who would build
On dreaming in this century of light?
Why, Stiver had a dream the other night;
There came a letter singularly sealed—

MRS STRAWMAN.

Its *treasure* such a dream prognosticates.

MISS JAY (*nodding*).

Yes, and next day they sued him for the rates.

[*The ladies make a circle round Lind and go in conversation with him into the garden.*

STRAWMAN
(*continuing, to Anna, who faintly tries to escape*).

From these considerations, daughter mine,
From these considerations, buttressed all
With reason, morals, and the Word Divine,
You now perceive that to desert your Call
Were absolutely inexcusable.

ANNA (*half crying*).

Oh! I'm so young—

STRAWMAN.

And it is natural,
I own, that one should hesitate to thrid
These perils, dare the snares that there lie hid;
From doubt's entanglement you must break free,—
Be of good cheer and follow Moll and me!

MRS STRAWMAN.

Yes, your dear mother tells me that I too
Was just as inconsolable as you
When we received our Call—

STRAWMAN.

And for like cause—
The fascination of the town—it was;
But when a little money had come in,
And the first pairs of infants, twin by twin,
She quite got over it.

FALK (*sotto voce to Strawman*).

Bravo, you able
Persuader.

STRAWMAN
(*Nodding to him and turning again to Anna*).

Now you've promised me, be stable.
Shall man renounce his work? Falk says the Call
Is not so very slender after all.
Did you not, Falk?

FALK.

Nay, pastor—

STRAWMAN.

To be sure—!

[*To Anna.*

Of something then at least you are secure.
What's gained by giving up, if that is so?
Look back into the ages long ago,
See, Adam, Eve—the Ark, see, pair by pair,
Birds in the field—the lilies in the air,
The little birds—the little birds—the fishes—
(*continues in a lower tone, as he withdraws with Anna*).

[*Miss Jay and the Aunts return with Lind.*

FALK.

Hurrah! Here come the veterans in array;
The old guard charging to retrieve the day!

MISS JAY.

Ah, in exact accordance with our wishes!

[*Aside.*

We *have* him, Falk!—Now let us tackle *her!*

[*Approaches Anna.*

STRAWMAN (*with a deprecating motion*).

She needs no secular solicitation;
The Spirit has spoken, what can Earth bestead—?

[*Modestly.*

If in some small degree my words have sped,
Power was vouchsafed me—!

MRS HALM.

Come, no more evasion,

Bring them together!

AUNTS (*with emotion*).

Ah, how exquisite!

STRAWMAN.

Yes, can there be a heart so dull and dead
As not to be entranced at such a sight!
It is so thrilling and so penetrating,
So lacerating, so exhilarating,
To see an innocent babe devoutly lay
Its offering on Duty's altar.

MRS HALM.

Nay,
Her family have also done their part.

MISS JAY.

I and the Aunts—I should imagine so.
You, Lind, may have the key to Anna's heart,
[*Presses his hand.*
But we possess a picklock, you must know,
Able to open where the key avails not.
And if in years to come, cares throng and thwart,
Only apply to us, our friendship fails not.

MRS HALM.

Yes, we shall hover round you all your life,—

MISS JAY.

And shield you from the fiend of wedded strife.

STRAWMAN.

Enchanting group! Love, friendship, hour of gladness,

Yet so pathetically touched with sadness.

[*Turning to Lind.*

But now, young man, pray make an end of this.

[*Leading Anna to him.*

Take thy betrothed—receive her—with a kiss!

LIND (*giving his hand to Anna*).

I stay at home!

ANNA (*at the same moment*).

I go with you!

ANNA (*amazed*).

You stay?

LIND (*equally so*).

You go with me?

ANNA (*with a helpless glance at the company*).

Why, then, we are divided as before!

LIND.

What's this?

THE LADIES.

What now?

MISS JAY (*excitedly*).

Our wills are all at war—

STRAWMAN.

She gave her solemn word to cross the sea
With him!

MISS JAY.

And he gave his to stay ashore
With her!

FALK (*laughing*).

They both complied; what would you more!

STRAWMAN.

These complications are too much for me.

[*Goes towards the background.*

AUNTS (*to one another*).

How in the world came they to disagree?

MRS HALM

(*To Guldstad and Stiver, who have been walking in the garden and now approach*).

The spirit of discord's in possession here.

[*Talks aside to them.*

MRS STRAWMAN

(*To Miss Jay, noticing that the table is being laid*).

There comes the tea.

MISS JAY (*curtly*).

Thank heaven.

FALK.

Hurrah! a cheer
For love and friendship, maiden aunts and tea!

STIVER.

But if the case stands thus, the whole proceeding

May easily be ended with a laugh;
All turns upon a single paragraph,
Which bids the wife attend the spouse. No pleading
Can wrest an ordinance so clearly stated—

MISS JAY.

Doubtless, but does that help us to agree?

STRAWMAN.

She must obey a law that heaven dictated.

STIVER.

But Lind can circumvent that law, you see.

[*To Lind.*

Put off your journey, and then—budge no jot.

AUNTS (*delighted*).

Yes, that's the way!

MRS HALM.

Agreed!

MISS JAY.

That cuts the knot.

[*Svanhild and the maids have meantime laid the tea-table beside the verandah steps. At Mrs Halm's invitation the ladies sit down. The rest of the company take their places, partly on the verandah and the summer-house, partly in the garden. Falk sits on the verandah. During the following scene they drink tea.*

MRS HALM (*smiling*).

And so our little storm is overblown.
Such summer showers do good when they are gone ;
The sunshine greets us with a double boon,
And promises a cloudless afternoon.

MISS JAY.

Ah yes, Love's blossom without rainy skies
Would never thrive according to our wishes.

FALK.

In dry land set it, and it forthwith dies ;
For in so far the flowers are like the fishes—

SVANHILD.

Nay, for Love lives, you know, upon the air—

MISS JAY.

Which is the death of fishes—

FALK.

So I say.

MISS JAY.

Aha, we've put a bridle on you there !

MRS STRAWMAN.

The tea is good, one knows by the bouquet.

FALK.

Well, let us keep the simile you chose.
Love is a flower ; for if heaven's blessed rain
Fall short, it all but pines to death— [*Pauses.*

MISS JAY.

What then ?

FALK (*with a gallant bow*).

Then come the aunts with the reviving hose.—
But poets have this simile employed,
And men for scores of centuries enjoyed,—
Yet hardly one its secret sense has hit;
For flowers are manifold and infinite.
Say, then, what flower is love? Name me, who knows,
The flower most like it?

MISS JAY.

Why, it is the rose;
Good gracious, that's exceedingly well known;—
Love, all agree, lends life a rosy tone.

A YOUNG LADY.

It is the snowdrop; growing, snow enfurled;
Till it peer forth, undreamt of by the world.

AN AUNT.

It is the dandelion,—made robust
By dint of human heel and horse hoof thrust;
Nay, shooting forth afresh when it is smitten,
As Pedersen so charmingly has written.

LIND.

It is the bluebell,—ringing in for all
Young hearts life's joyous Whitsun festival.

MRS HALM.

No, 'tis an evergreen,—as fresh and gay
In desolate December as in May.

GULDSTAD.

No, Iceland moss, dry gathered,—far the best
Cure for young ladies with a wounded breast.

A GENTLEMAN.

No, the wild chestnut tree,—in high repute
For household fuel, but with a bitter fruit.

SVANHILD.

No, a camelia; at our balls, 'tis said,
The chief adornment of a lady's head.

MRS STRAWMAN.

No, it is like a flower, O such a bright one;—
Stay now—a blue one, no, it was a white one—
What *is* its name—? Dear me—the one I met—;
Well it is singular how I forget!

STIVER.

None of these flower similitudes will run.
The flower*pot* is a likelier candidate.
There's only room in it, at once, for *one*,
But by progressive stages it holds *eight*.

STRAWMAN (*with his little girls round him*).

No, love's a pear tree; in the spring like snow
With myriad blossoms, which in summer grow
To pearlets; in the parent's sap each shares;—
And with God's help they'll all alike prove pears.

FALK.

So many heads, so many sentences!

No, you all grope and blunder off the line.
Each simile's at fault; I'll tell you mine;—
You're free to turn and wrest it as you please.
[*Rises as if to make a speech.*
In the remotest east there grows a plant;
And the sun's cousin's garden is its haunt—

THE LADIES.

Ah, it's the tea-plant!

FALK.

Yes.

MRS STRAWMAN.

His voice is so
Like Strawman's when he—

STRAWMAN.

Don't disturb his flow.

FALK.

It has its home in fabled lands serene;
Thousands of miles of desert lie between;—
Fill up, Lind!—So.—Now in a tea-oration,
I'll show of tea and Love the true relation,
[*The guests cluster round him.*
It has its home in the romantic land;
Alas, Love's home is also in Romance,
Only the Sun's descendants understand
The herb's right cultivation and advance.
With Love it is not otherwise than so.
Blood of the Sun along the veins must flow
If Love indeed therein is to strike root,
And burgeon into blossom, into fruit.

MISS JAY.

But China is an ancient land; you hold
In consequence that tea is very old—

STRAWMAN.

Past question antecedent to Jerusalem.

FALK.

Yes, 'twas already famous when Methusalem
His picture-books and rattles tore and flung—

MISS JAY (*triumphantly*).

And Love is in its very nature young!
To find a likeness there is pretty bold.

FALK.

No; Love, in truth, is also very old;
That principle we here no more dispute
Than do the folks of Rio or Beyrout.
Nay, there are those from Cayenne to Caithness,
Who stand upon its everlastingness;—
Well, that may be a slight exaggeration,
But old it is beyond all estimation.

MISS JAY.

But Love is all alike; whereas we see
Both good and bad and middling kinds of tea!

MRS STRAWMAN.

Yes, they sell tea of many qualities.

ANNA.

The green spring shoots I count the very first—

SVANHILD.

Those serve to quench celestial daughters' thirst.

A YOUNG LADY.

Witching as ether fumes they say it is—

ANOTHER.

Balmy as lotus, sweet as almond, clear—

GULDSTAD.

That's not an article we deal in here.

FALK

(*Who has meanwhile come down from the verandah*).

Ah, ladies, every mortal has a small
Private celestial empire in his heart.
There bud such shoots in thousands, kept apart
By Shyness's soon shatter'd Chinese Wall.
But in her dim fantastic temple bower
The little Chinese puppet sits and sighs,
A dream of far-off wonders in her eyes—
And in her hand a golden tulip flower.
For *her* the tender firstling tendrils grew;—
Rich crop or meagre, what is that to you?
Instead of it we get an after crop
They kick the tree for, dust and stalk and stem,—
As hemp to silk beside what goes to them—

GULDSTAD.

That is the black tea.

FALK (*nodding*).

That's what fills the shop.

A GENTLEMAN.

There's beef tea too, that Holberg says a word of—

MISS JAY (*sharply*).

To modern taste entirely out of date.

FALK.

And a *beef love* has equally been heard of,
Wont—in romances—to brow-beat its mate,
And still they say its trace may be detected
Amongst the henpecked of the married state.
In short there's likeness where 'twas least expected.
So, as you know, an ancient proverb tells,
That something ever passes from the tea
Of the bouquet that lodges in its cells,
If it be carried hither over sea.
It must across the desert and the hills,—
Pay toll to Cossack and to Russian tills;—
It gets their stamp and licence, that's enough,
We buy it as the true and genuine stuff.
But has not Love the selfsame path to fare?
Across Life's desert? How the world would rave
And shriek if you or I should boldly bear
Our Love by way of Freedom's ocean wave!
"Good heavens, his moral savour's passed away,
"And quite dispersed Legality's bouquet!"—

STRAWMAN (*rising*).

Yes, happily,— in every moral land
Such wares continue to be contraband!

FALK.

Yes, to pass current here, Love must have cross'd
The great Siberian waste of regulations,
Fann'd by no breath of ocean to its cost;
It must produce official attestations
From friends and kindred, devils of relations,
From church curators, organist and clerk,
And other fine folks—over and above
The primal licence which God gave to Love.—
And then the last great point of likeness;—mark
How heavily the hand of culture weighs
Upon that far Celestial domain;
Its power is shatter'd, and its wall decays,
The last true Mandarin's strangled; hands profane
Already are put forth to share the spoil;
Soon the Sun's realm will be a legend vain,
An idle tale incredible to sense;
The world is gray in gray—we've flung the soil
On buried Faery,—we have made her mound.
But if we have,—then where can Love be found?
Alas, Love also is departed hence! [*Lifts his cup.*
Well let him go, since so the times decree;—
A health to Amor, late of Earth,—in tea!

[*He drains his cup; indignant murmurs amongst the company.*

MISS JAY.

A very odd expression! "Dead" indeed!

THE LADIES.

To say that Love is dead—!

STRAWMAN.

Why, here you see
Him sitting, rosy, round and sound, at tea,
In all conditions! Here in her sable weed
The widow—

MISS JAY.

Here a couple, true and tried,—

STIVER.

With many ample pledges fortified.

GULDSTAD.

Then Love's light cavalry, of maid and man,
The plighted pairs in order—

STRAWMAN.

In the van
The veterans, whose troth has laughed to scorn
The tooth of Time—

MISS JAY (*hastily interrupting*).

And then the babes new-born—
The little novices of yester-morn—

STRAWMAN.

Spring, summer, autumn, winter, in a word,
Are here; the truth is patent, past all doubt,
It can be clutched and handled, seen and heard,—

FALK.

What then?

MISS JAY.

And yet you want to thrust it out!

FALK.

Madam, you quite mistake. In all I spoke
I cast no doubt on anything you claim;
But I would fain remind you that, from smoke,
We cannot logically argue flame.
That men are married, and have children, I
Have no desire whatever to deny;
Nor do I dream of doubting that such things
Are in the world as troth and wedding-rings;
That billets-doux some tender hands indite
And seal with pairs of turtle doves that—fight;
That sweethearts swarm in cottage and in hall,
That chocolate rewards the wedding-call;
That usage and convention have decreed,
In every point, how "Lovers" shall proceed:—
But, heavens! We've majors also by the score,
Arsenals heaped with muniments of war,
With spurs and howitzers and drums and shot,
But what does that permit us to infer?
That we have men who dangle swords, but not
That they will wield the weapons that they wear.
Tho' all the plain with gleaming tents you crowd,
Does that make heroes of the men they shroud?

STRAWMAN.

Well, all in moderation; I must own,
It is not quite conducive to the truth
That we should paint the enamourment of youth
So bright, as if—ahem—it stood alone.

Love-making still a frail foundation is.
Only the snuggery of wedded bliss
Provides a rock where Love may builded be
In unassailable security.

MISS JAY.

There I entirely differ. In my view,
A free accord of lovers, heart with heart,
Who hold together, having leave to part,
Gives the best warrant that their love is true.

ANNA (*warmly*).

O no—Love's bond when it is fresh and young
Is of a stuff more precious and more strong.

LIND (*thoughtfully*).

Possibly the ideal flower may blow,
Even as that snowdrop,—hidden by the snow.

FALK (*with a sudden outburst*).

You fallen Adam! There a heart was cleft
With longing for the Eden it has left!

LIND.

What stuff!

MRS HALM (*offended, to Falk, rising*).

'Tis not a very friendly act
To stir a quarrel where we've made a peace.
As for your friend's good fortune, be at ease—

SOME LADIES.

Nay that's assured—

OTHERS.

A very certain fact.

MRS HALM.

The cooking-class at school, I must confess,
She did not take ; but she shall learn it still.

MISS JAY.

With her own hands she's trimming her own dress

AN AUNT (*patting Anna's hand*).

And growing exquisitely sensible.

FALK (*laughing aloud*).

O parody of sense, that rives and rends
In maniac dance upon the lips of friends!
Was it good sense he wanted? Or a she-
Professor of the lore of Cookery?
A joyous son of springtime he came here,
For the wild rosebud on the bush he burned.
You reared the rosebud for him ; he returned—
And for his rose found what? The hip!

MISS JAY (*offended*).

You jeer!

FALK.

A useful household condiment, heaven knows!
But yet the hip was not his bridal rose.

MRS HALM.

O, if it is a ball-room queen he wants,
I'm very sorry ; these are not their haunts.

FALK.

O yes, I know the pretty coquetry
They carry on with "Domesticity."
It is a suckling of the mighty Lie
That, like hop-tendrils, spreads itself on high.
I, madam, reverently bare my head
To the ball queen ; a child of beauty she—
And the ideal's golden woof is spread
In ball-rooms, hardly in the nursery.

MRS HALM (*with suppressed bitterness*).

Your conduct, sir, is easily explained ;
A plighted lover cannot be a friend ;
That is the kernel of the whole affair ;
I have a very large experience there.

FALK.

No doubt,—with seven nieces, each a wife—

MRS HALM.

And each a happy wife—

FALK (*with emphasis*).

Ah, do we know ?

GULDSTAD.

How !

MISS JAY.

Mr Falk !

LIND.

Are you resolved to sow

Dissension?

FALK (*vehemently*).

Yes, war, discord, turmoil, strife!

STIVER.

What you, a lay, profane outsider here!

FALK.

No matter, still the battle-flag I'll rear!
Yes, it is war I mean with nail and tooth
Against the Lie with the tenacious root,
The lie that you have fostered into fruit,
For all its strutting in the guise of truth!

STIVER.

Against these groundless charges I protest,
Reserving right of action—

MISS JAY.

Do be still!

FALK.

So then it is Love's ever-running rill
That tells the widow what she once possess'd,—
That Love that, in the happy days gone by,
Out of her language blotted "moan" and "sigh"!
So then it is Love's brimming tide that rolls
Along the placid veins of wedded souls,—
That Love that fiercely faced the iron sleet,
Trampling inane Convention under feet,
And scoffing at the impotent discreet!

So then it is Love's beauty-kindled flame
That keeps the plighted from the taint of time
Year after year! Ah yes, the very same
That made our young bureaucrat blaze in rhyme!
So it is Love's young bliss that will not brave
The voyage over vaulted Ocean's wave,
But asks a sacrifice when, like the sun,
Its face should fill with glory, *making* one!
Ah no, you vulgar prophets of the Lie,
Give things the names we ought to know them by;
Call widows' passion—wanting what they miss,
And wedlock's *habit*—call it what it is!

STRAWMAN.

Young man, this insolence has gone too far!
In every word there's scoffing and defiance.

[*Goes close up to Falk.*

Now I'll gird up my aged loins to war
For hallowed custom against modern science!

FALK.

I go to battle as it were a feast!

STRAWMAN.

Good! For your bullets I will be a beacon!—

[*Nearer.*

A wedded pair is holy, like a priest—

STIVER (*at Falk's other side*).

And a betrothed—

FALK.

Half-holy, like the deacon.

STRAWMAN.

Behold these children ;—see,—this little throng !
Io triumphe may for them be sung !
How was it possible—how practicable—;
The words of truth are strong, inexorable ;—
He has no hearing whom they cannot move.
See,—every one of them's a child of Love— !

[*Stops in confusion.*

That is—you understand—I would have said— !

MISS JAY (*fanning herself with her handkerchief*).

This is a very mystical oration !

FALK.

There you yourself provide the demonstration,—
A good old Norse one, sound, true-born, home-bred.
You draw distinction between wedded pledges
And those of Love : your Logic's without flaw.
They are distinguished just as roast from raw,
As hothouse bloom from wilding of the hedges !
Love is with us a science and an art ;
It long since ceased to animate the heart.
Love is with us a trade, a special line
Of business, with its union, code and sign ;
It is a guild of married folks and plighted,
Past-masters with apprentices united ;
For they cohere compact as jelly-fishes,
A singing-club their single want and wish is—

GULDSTAD.

And a gazette !

FALK.

A good suggestion, yes!
We too must have our organ in the press,
Like ladies, athletes, boys, and devotees.
Don't ask the price at present, if you please.
There I'll parade each amatory fetter
That John and Thomas to our town unites,
There publish every pink and perfumed letter
That William to his tender Jane indites;
There you shall read, among "Distressing Scenes"—
Instead of murders and burnt crinolines,
The broken matches that the week's afforded;
There under "goods for sale" you'll find what firms
Will furnish cast-off rings on easy terms;
There double, treble births will be recorded;
No wedding, but our rallying rub-a-dub
Shall drum to the performance all the club;
No suit rejected, but we'll set it down,
In letters large, with other news of weight
Thus: "Amor-Moloch, we regret to state,
Has claimed another victim in our town."
You'll see, we'll catch subscribers: once in sight
Of the propitious season when they bite,
By way of throwing them the bait they'll brook
I'll stick a nice young man upon my hook.
Yes, you will see me battle for your cause,
With tiger's, nay with editorial, claws
Rending them—

GULDSTAD.

And the paper's name will be—?

FALK.

Amor's Norse Chronicle of Archery.

STIVER (*going nearer*).

You're not in earnest, you will never stake
Your name and fame for such a fancy's sake!

FALK.

I'm in grim earnest. We are often told
Men cannot live on love; I'll show that this
Is an untenable hypothesis;
For Love will prove to be a mine of gold:
Particularly if Miss Jay, perhaps,
Will Mr Strawman's "Life's Romance" unfold,
As appetising feuilleton, in scraps.

STRAWMAN (*in terror*).

Merciful heaven! My "life's romance!" What, what!
When was my life romantic, if you please?

MISS JAY.

I never said so.

STIVER.

Witness disagrees.

STRAWMAN.

That I have ever swerved a single jot
From social prescript,—is a monstrous lie.

FALK.

Good.

[*Clapping Stiver on the shoulder.*

Here's a friend who will not put me by.
We'll start with Stiver's lyric ecstacies.

STIVER (*after a glance of horror at Strawman*).

Are you quite mad! Nay then I must be heard!
You dare accuse me for a poet—

MISS JAY.

How—!

FALK.

Your office has averred it anyhow.

STIVER (*in towering anger*).

Sir, by our office nothing is averred.

FALK.

Well, leave me then, you also: I have by me
One comrade yet whose loyalty will last.
"A true heart's story" Lind will not deny me,
Whose troth's too tender for the ocean blast,
Who for his mistress makes surrender of
His fellow-men—pure quintessence of Love!

MRS HALM.

My patience, Mr Falk, is now worn out.
The same abode no longer can receive us:—
I beg of you this very day to leave us—

FALK

(*with a bow as Mrs Halm and the company withdraw*).

That this would come I never had a doubt!

STRAWMAN.

Between us two there's battle to the death;
You've slandered me, my wife, my little flock,
From Molly down to Millie, in one breath.
Crow on, crow on—Emancipation's cock,—
[*goes in, followed by his wife and children.*

FALK.

And go you on observing Peter's faith
To Love your lord—who, thanks to your advice,
Was thrice denied before the cock crew thrice!

MISS JAY (*turning faint*).

Attend me, Stiver! help me get unlaced
My corset—this way, this way—do make haste!

STIVER
(*to Falk as he withdraws with Miss Jay on his arm*).

I here renounce your friendship.

LIND.

I likewise.

FALK (*seriously*).

You too, my Lind?

LIND.

Farewell.

FALK.

You were my nearest one—

LIND.

No help, it is the pleasure of my dearest one.

[*He goes in: Svanhild has remained standing on the verandah steps.*

FALK.

So, now I've made a clearance, have free course
In all directions!

SVANHILD.

Falk, one word with you!

FALK (*pointing politely to the house*).

That way, Miss Halm;—that way, with all the force
Of aunts and inmates, Mrs Halm withdrew.

SVANHILD (*nearer to him*).

Let them withdraw; their ways and mine divide;
I will not swell the number of their band.

FALK.

You'll stay?

SVANHILD.

If you make war on lies, I stand
A trusty armour-bearer by your side.

FALK.

You, Svanhild, you who—

SVANHILD.

I, who—yesterday—?
Were you yourself, Falk, yesterday the same?
You bade me be a sallow, for your play.

FALK.

And a sweet sallow sang me into shame.
No, you are right: I was a child to ask;
But you have fired me to a nobler task.
Right in the midst of men the Church is founded
Where Truth's appealing clarion must be sounded
We are not called, like demigods, to gaze on
The battle from the far-off mountain's crest,
But in our hearts to bear our fiery blazon,
An Olaf's cross upon a mailed breast,—
To look afar across the fields of fight,
Tho' pent within the mazes of its might,—
Beyond the mirk descry one glimmer still
Of glory—that's the Call we must fulfil.

SVANHILD.

And you'll fulfil it when you break from men,
Stand free, alone,—

FALK.

Did I frequent them *then?*
And there lies duty. No, that time's gone by,—
My solitary compact with the sky.
My four-wall-chamber poetry is done;
My verse shall live in forest and in field,
I'll fight under the splendour of the sun;—
I or the Lie—one of us two must yield!

SVANHILD.

Then forth with God from Verse to Derring-doe!
I did you wrong: you have a feeling heart;
Forgive me,—and as good friends let us part—

FALK.

Nay, in my future there is room for two!
We part not. Svanhild, if you dare decide,
We'll battle on together side by side.

SVANHILD.

We battle?

FALK.

See, I have no friend, no mate,
By all abandoned, I make war on all:
At me they aim the piercing shafts of hate;
Say, do you dare with me to stand or fall?
Henceforth along the beaten walks I'll move
Heedful of each constraining etiquette;
Spread, like the rest of men, my board, and set
The ring upon the finger of my love!
[*Takes a ring from his finger and holds it up.*

SVANHILD (*in breathless suspense*).

You mean *that*?

FALK.

Yes, by us the world shall see,
Love has an everlasting energy,
That suffers not its splendour to take hurt
From the day's dust, the common highway's dirt.
Last night I showed you the ideal aflame,
Beaconing from a dizzy mountain's brow.
You shuddered, for you were a woman,—now
I show you woman's veritable aim;—
A soul like yours, what it has vowed, will keep.
You see the abyss before you,—Svanhild, leap!

SVANHILD (*almost inaudibly*).

If we should fail—!

FALK (*exulting*).

No, in your eyes I see
A gleam that surely prophesies our winning!

SVANHILD.

Then take me as I am, take all of me!
Now buds the young leaf; now my spring's beginning!

[*She flings herself boldly into his arms as the curtain falls.*

ACT III.

Evening. Bright moonlight. Coloured lanterns are hung about the trees. In the background are covered tables with bottles, glasses, biscuits, etc. From the house, which is lighted up from top to bottom, subdued music and singing are heard during the following scene. Svanhild stands on the verandah. FALK *comes from the right with some books and a portfolio under his arm. The* PORTER *follows with a portmanteau and a knapsack.*

FALK.

That's all, then?

PORTER.

Yes, sir, all is in the pack,
But just a satchel, and the paletot.

FALK.

Good; when I go, I'll take them on my back.
Now off. See, this is the portfolio.

PORTER.

It's locked, I see.

FALK.

Locked, Peter.

PORTER.

Good, sir.

FALK.

Pray,

Make haste and burn it.

PORTER.

Burn it?

FALK

Yes, to ash—

[*Smiling.*

With every draft upon poetic cash;
As for the books, you're welcome to them.

PORTER.

Nay,

Such payment is above a poor man's earning.
But, sir, I'm thinking, if you can bestow
Your books, you must have done with all your learning?

FALK.

Whatever can be learnt from books I know,
And rather more.

PORTER.

More? Nay, that's hard, I doubt!

FALK.

Well, now be off; the carriers wait without.
Just help them load the barrow ere you go.
[*The Porter goes out to the left.*

FALK (*approaching Svanhild who comes to meet him*).

One moment's ours, my Svanhild, in the light
Of God and of the lustrous summer night.
How the stars glitter thro' the leafage, see,
Like bright fruit hanging on the great world-tree.
Now slavery's last manacle I slip,
Now for the last time feel the wealing whip;
Like Israel at the Passover I stand,
Loins girded for the desert, staff in hand.
Dull generation, from whose sight is hid
The Promised Land beyond that desert flight,
Thrall tricked with knighthood, never the more knight,
Tomb thyself kinglike in the Pyramid,—
I cross the barren desert to be free.
My ship strides on despite an ebbing sea;
But there the Legion Lie shall find its doom,
And glut one deep, dark, hollow-vaulted tomb.
[*A short pause; he looks at her and takes her hand.*
You are so still!

SVANHILD.

So happy! Suffer me,
O suffer me in silence still to dream.
Speak you for me; my budding thoughts, grown strong,
One after one will burgeon into song,
Like lilies in the bosom of the stream.

FALK.

O say it once again, in truth's pure tone
Beyond the fear of doubt, that thou art mine!
O say it, Svanhild, say—

SVANHILD (*throwing herself on his neck*).

Yes, I am thine!

FALK.

Thou singing-bird God sent me for my own!

SVANHILD.

Homeless within my mother's house I dwelt,
Lonely in all I thought, in all I felt,
A guest unbidden at the feast of mirth,—
Accounted nothing—less than nothing—worth.
Then you appeared! For the first time I heard
My own thought uttered in another's word;
To my lame visions you gave wings and feet—
You young unmasker of the Obsolete!
Half with your caustic keenness you alarmed me,
Half with your radiant eloquence you charmed me,
As sea-girt forests summon with their spell
The sea their flinty beaches still repel.
Now I have read the bottom of your soul,
Now you have won me, undivided, whole;
Dear forest, where my tossing billows beat,
My tide's at flood and never will retreat!

FALK.

And I thank God that in the bath of Pain

He purged my love. What strong compulsion drew
Me on I knew not, till I saw in you
The treasure I had blindly sought in vain.
I praise Him, who our love has lifted thus
To noble rank by sorrow,—licensed us
To a triumphal progress, bade us sweep
Thro' fen and forest to our castle-keep,
A noble pair, astride on Pegasus!

SVANHILD (*pointing to the house*).

The whole house, see, is making feast to-night.
There, in their honour, every room's alight,
There cheerful talk and joyous song ring out;
On the highroad no passer-by will doubt
That men are happy where they are so gay.
[*With compassion.*
Poor sister!—happy in the great world's way!

FALK.

"Poor" sister, say you?

SVANHILD.

Has she not divided
With kith and kin the treasure of her soul,
Her capital to fifty hands confided,
So that not one is debtor for the whole?
From no one has she *all* things to receive,
For no one has she utterly to live.
O beside *my* wealth hers is little worth;
I have but one possession upon earth.
My heart was lordless when with trumpet blare
And multitudinous song you came, its king,

The banners of my thought your ensign bear,
You fill my soul with glory, like the spring.
Yes, I must needs thank God, when it is past,
That I was lonely till I found out thee,—
That I lay dead until the trumpet blast
Waken'd me from the world's frivolity.

FALK.

Yes we, who have no friends on earth, we twain
Own the true wealth, the golden fortune,—we
Who stand without, beside the starlit sea,
And watch the indoor revel thro' the pane.
Let the lamp glitter and the song resound,
Let the dance madly eddy round and round;—
Look up, my Svanhild, into yon deep blue,—
There glitter little lamps in thousands, too—

SVANHILD.

And hark, beloved, thro' the limes there floats
This balmy eve a chorus of sweet notes—

FALK.

It is for us that fretted vault 's aglow—

SVANHILD.

It is for us the vale is loud below!

FALK.

I feel myself like God's lost prodigal;
I left Him for the world's delusive charms.
With mild reproof He wooed me to his arms;
And when I come, He lights the vaulted hall,

Prepares a banquet for the son restored,
And makes His noblest creature my reward.
From this time forth I'll never leave that Light,—
But stand its armed defender in the fight;
Nothing shall part us, and our life shall prove
A song of glory to triumphant love!

SVANHILD.

And see how easy triumph is for two,
When he's a man—

FALK.

She, woman thro' and thro';—
It is impossible for such to fall!

SVANHILD.

Then up, and to the war with want and sorrow;
This very hour I will declare it all!
[*Pointing to Falk's ring on her finger.*

FALK *hastily*).

No, Svanhild, not to-night, wait till to-morrow!
To-night we gather our young love's red rose;
'Twere sacrilege to smirch it with the prose
Of common day.
[*The door into the garden room opens.*
Your mother's coming! Hide!
No eye this night shall see thee as my bride!
[*They go out among the trees by the summer-house. Mrs Halm and Guldstad come out on the balcony.*

MRS HALM.

He's really going

GULDSTAD.

Seems so, I admit.

STIVER (*coming*).

He's going, madam!

MRS HALM.

We're aware of it!

STIVER.

A most unfortunate punctilio.
He'll keep his word; his stubbornness I know.
In the Gazette he'll put us all by name;
My love will figure under leaded headings,
With jilts, and twins, and countermanded weddings.
Listen; I tell you, if it weren't for shame,
I would propose an armistice, a truce—

MRS HALM.

You think he would be willing?

STIVER.

I deduce
The fact from certain signs, which indicate
That his tall talk about his Amor's News
Was uttered in a far from sober state.
One proof especially, if not transcendent,
Yet tells most heavily against defendant:
It has been clearly proved that after dinner
To his and Lind's joint chamber he withdrew,
And there displayed such singular demeanour
As leaves no question—

GULDSTAD.

[*Sees a glimpse of Falk and Svanhild, who separate, Falk going to the background ; Svanhild remains standing hidden by the summer-house.*

Hold, we have the clue!
Madam, one word!—Falk does not mean to go,
Or if he does, he means it as a friend.

STIVER.

How, you believe then—?

MRS HALM.

What do you intend?

GULDSTAD.

With the least possible delay I'll show
That matters move precisely as you would.
Merely a word in private—

MRS HALM.

Very good.

[*They go together into the garden and are seen from time to time in lively conversation.*

STIVER

(*Descending into the garden discovers Falk, who is standing by the water and gazing over it*).

These poets are mere men of vengeance, we
State servants understand diplomacy.
I need to labour for myself—

[*Seeing* STRAWMAN, *who enters from the garden room.*

Well met!

STRAWMAN (*on the verandah*).

He's really leaving! [*Going down to Stiver.*
Ah, my dear sir, let
Me beg you just a moment to go in
And hold my wife—

STIVER.

I—hold her, sir?

STRAWMAN.

I mean
In talk. The little ones and we are so
Unused to be divided, there is no
Escaping—
[*His wife and children appear in the door.*
Ha! already on my trail.

MRS STRAWMAN.

Where are you, Strawman?

STRAWMAN (*aside to Stiver*).

Do invent some tale,
Something amusing—something to beguile!

STIVER (*going on to the verandah*).

Pray, madam, have you read the official charge?
A masterpiece of literary style.
[*Takes a book from his pocket.*
Which I shall now proceed to cite at large.
[*Ushers her politely into the room, and follows himself. Falk comes forward; he and Strawman meet; they regard one another a moment in silence.*

STRAWMAN.

Well?

FALK.

Well?

STRAWMAN.

Falk!

FALK.

Pastor!

STRAWMAN.

Are you less
Intractable than when we parted?

FALK.

Nay,
I go my own inexorable way—

STRAWMAN.

Even tho' you crush another's happiness?

FALK.

I plant the flower of knowledge in its place.

[*Smiling.*

If, by the way, you have not ceased to think
Of the Gazette—

STRAWMAN.

Ah, that was all a joke?

FALK.

Yes, pluck up courage, that will turn to smoke;
I break the ice in action, not in ink.

STRAWMAN.

But even though you spare me, sure enough
There's one who won't so lightly let me off;
He has the advantage, and he won't forego it,
That lawyer's clerk—and 'tis to you I owe it;
You raked the ashes of our faded flames,
And you may take your oath he won't be still
If once I mutter but a syllable
Against the brazen bluster of his claims.
These civil-service gentlemen, they say,
Are very potent in the press to-day.
A trumpery paragraph can lay me low,
Once printed in that Samson-like Gazette
That with the jaw of asses fells its foe,
And runs away with tackle and with net,
Especially towards the quarter day—

FALK (*acquiescing*).

Ah, were there scandal in the case, indeed—

STRAWMAN (*despondently*).

No matter. Read its columns with good heed,
You'll see me offered up to Vengeance.

FALK (*whimsically*).

Nay,

To retribution—well-earned punishment.
Thro' all our life there runs a Nemesis,
Which may delay, but never will relent,
And grants to none exception or release.
Who wrongs the Ideal? Straight there rushes in

The Press, its guardian with the Argus eye,
And the offender suffers for his sin.

STRAWMAN.

But in the name of heaven, what pledge have I
Given this "Ideal" that's ever on your tongue?
I'm married, have a family, twelve young
And helpless innocents to clothe and keep;
I have my daily calls on every side,
Churches remote and glebe and pasture wide,
Great herds of breeding cattle, ghostly sheep—
All to be watched and cared for, clipt and fed,
Grain to be winnowed, compost to be spread;—
Wanted all day in shippon and in stall,
What time have *I* to serve the "Ideal" withal?

FALK.

Then get you home with what dispatch you may,
Creep snugly in before the winter-cold;
Look, in young Norway dawns at last the day,
Thousand brave hearts are in its ranks enroll'd,
Its banners in the morning breezes play!

STRAWMAN.

And if, young man, I were to take my way
With bag and baggage home, with everything
What made me yesterday a little king,
Were mine the only *volte face* to-day?
Think you I carry back the wealth I brought?
[*As Falk is about to answer.*
Nay, listen, let me first explain my thought.
[*Coming nearer.*

Time was when I was young, like you, and played
Like you, the unconquerable Titan's part;
Year after year I toiled and moiled for bread,
Which hardens a man's hand, but not his heart.
For northern fells my lonely home surrounded,
And by my parish bounds my world was bounded.
My home—Ah, Falk, I wonder, do you know
What home is?

FALK (*curtly*).

I have never known.

STRAWMAN.

Just so.
That is a home, where five may dwell with ease,
Tho' two would be a crowd, if enemies.
That is a home, where all your thoughts play free
As boys and girls about their father's knee,
Where speech no sooner touches heart, than tongue
Darts back an answering harmony of song;
Where you may grow from flax-haired snowy-polled,
And not a soul take note that you grow old;
Where memories grow fairer as they fade,
Like far blue peaks beyond the forest glade.

FALK (*with constrained sarcasm*).

Come, you grow warm—

STRAWMAN.

Where you but jeered and flouted.
So utterly unlike God made us two!
I'm bare of that he lavished upon you.

But I have won the game where you were routed.
Seen from the clouds, full many a wayside grain
Of truth seems empty chaff and husks. You'd soar
To heaven, I scarcely reach the stable door,
One bird's an eagle born—

FALK.

And one a hen.

STRAWMAN.

Yes, laugh away, and say it be so, grant
I am a hen. There clusters to my cluck
A crowd of little chickens,—which you want!
And I've the hen's high spirit and her pluck,
And for my little ones forget myself.
You think me dull, I know it. Possibly
You pass a harsher judgment yet, decree
Me over covetous of worldly pelf.
Good, on that head we will not disagree.

[*Seizes Falk's arm and continues in a low tone but with gathering vehemence.*

You're right, I'm dull and dense and grasping, yes;
But grasping for my God-given babes and wife,
And dense from struggling blindly for bare life,
And dull from sailing seas of loneliness.
Just when the pinnace of my youthful dream
Into the everlasting deep went down,
Another started from the ocean stream
Borne with a fair wind onward to life's crown.
For every dream that vanished in the wave,
For every buoyant plume that broke asunder,

God sent me in return a little Wonder,
And gratefully I took the good He gave.
For them I strove, for them amassed, annexed,—
For them, for them, explained the Holy text;
My clustering girls, my garden of delight!
On them you've poured the venom of your spite!
You've proved, with all the cunning of the schools,
My bliss was but the paradise of fools,
That all I took for earnest was a jest;—
Now I implore, give me my quiet breast
Again, the flawless peace of mind I had—

FALK.

Prove, in a word, your title to be glad?

STRAWMAN.

Yes, in my path you've cast the stone of doubt,
And nobody but you can cast it out.
Between my kin and me you've set a bar,—
Remove the bar, the strangling noose undo—

FALK.

You possibly believe I keep the glue
Of lies for Happiness's broken jar?

STRAWMAN.

I do believe, the faith your reasons tore
To shreds, your reasons may again restore;
The limb that you have shatter'd, you can set;
Reverse your judgment,—the whole truth unfold,
Restate the case—I'll fly my banner yet—

FALK (*haughtily*).

I stamp no copper Happiness as gold.

STRAWMAN (*looking fixedly at him*).

Remember then that, lately, one whose scent
For truth is of the keenest told us this:

[*With uplifted finger.*

" There runs through all our life a Nemesis,
Which may delay, but never will relent."

[*He goes towards the house.*

STIVER

(*Coming out with glasses on, and an open book in his hand*).

Pastor, you must come flying like the blast!
Your girls are sobbing—

THE CHILDREN (*in the doorway*).

Pa!

STIVER.

And Madam waiting!

[*Strawman goes in.*

This lady has no talent for debating.

[*Puts the book and glasses in his pocket, and approaches Falk.*

Falk!

FALK.

Yes!

STIVER.

I hope you've changed your mind at last?

FALK.

Why so?

STIVER.

For obvious reasons. To betray
Communications made in confidence,
Is conduct utterly without defence.
They must not pass the lips.

FALK.

No, I've heard say
It is at times a risky game to play.

STIVER.

The very devil!

FALK.

Only for the great.

STIVER (*zealously*).

No, no, for all us servants of the state.
Only imagine how my future chances
Would dwindle, if the governor once knew
I keep a Pegasus that neighs and prances
In office hours—and such an office, too!
From first to last, you know, in our profession,
The winged horse is viewed with reprobation:
But worst of all would be, if it got wind
That I against our primal law had sinn'd
By bringing secret matters to the light—

FALK.

That's penal, is it—such an oversight?

STIVER (*mysteriously*).

It can a servant of the state compel
To beg for his dismissal out of hand.
On us officials lies a strict command,
Even by the hearth to be inscrutable.

FALK.

O those despotical authorities,
Muzzling the—clerk that treadeth out the grain!

STIVER (*shrugging his shoulders*).

It is the law; to murmur is in vain.
Moreover, at a moment such as this,
When salary revision is in train,
It is not well to advertise one's views
Of office time's true function and right use.
That's why I beg you to be silent; look,
A word may forfeit my—

FALK.

Portfolio?

STIVER.

Officially it's called a transcript book;
A protocol's the clasp upon the veil of snow
That shrouds the modest breast of the Bureau.
What lies beneath you must not seek to know.

FALK.

And yet I only spoke at your desire;
You hinted at your literary crop.

STIVER.

How should I guess he'd grovel in the mire
So deep, this parson perch'd on fortune's top,
A man with snug appointments, children, wife,
And money to defy the ills of life?
If such a man prove such a Philistine,
What shall of us poor copyists be said?
Of me, who drive the quill and rule the line,
A man engaged and shortly to be wed,
With family in prospect—and so forth?

[*More vehemently.*

O, if I only had a well-lined berth,
I'd bind the armour'd helmet on my head,
And cry defiance to united earth!
And were I only unengaged like you,
Trust me, I'd break a road athwart the snow
Of Prose, and carry the Ideal thro'!

FALK.

To work then, man!

STIVER.

How?

FALK.

You may still do so!
Let the world's prudish owl unheeded flutter by;
Freedom converts the grub into a butterfly!

STIVER (*stepping back*).

You mean, to break the engagement—?

FALK.

That's my mind;—
The fruit is gone, why keep the empty rind?

STIVER.

Such a proposal's for a green young shoot,
Not for a man of judgment and repute.
I heed not what King Christian in his time
(The Fifth) laid down about engagements broken-off;
For that relationship is nowhere spoken of
In any rubric of the code of crime.
The act would not be criminal in name,
It would in no way violate the laws—

FALK.

Why there, you see then!

STIVER (*firmly*).

Yes, but all the same,—
I must reject all pleas in such a cause.
Staunch comrades we have been in times of dearth;
Of life's disport she asks but little share,
And I'm a homely fellow, long aware
God made me for the ledger and the hearth.
Let others emulate the eagle's flight,
Life in the lowly plains may be as bright.
What does his Excellency Goethe say
About the white and shining milky way?
Man may not there the milk of fortune skim,
Nor is the butter of it meant for him.

FALK.

Why, even were fortune-churning our life's goal,

The labour must be guided by the soul;—
Be citizens of the time that is—but then
Make the time worthy of the citizen.
In homely things lurks beauty, without doubt,
But watchful eye and brain must draw it out.
Not every man who loves the soil he turns
May therefore claim to be another Burns.

STIVER.

Then let us each our proper path pursue,
And part in peace ; we shall not hamper you ;
We keep the road, you hover in the sky,
There where we too once floated, she and I.
But work, not song, provides our daily bread,
And when a man's alive, his music's dead.
A young man's life's a lawsuit, and the most
Superfluous litigation in existence :
Withdraw, make terms, abandon all resistance :
Plead where and how you will, your suit is lost.

FALK
(*Bold and confident, with a glance at the summer-house*).

Nay, tho' I took it to the highest place,—
Judgment, I know, would be reversed by grace !
I know two hearts can live a life complete,
With hope still ardent, and with faith still sweet ;
You preach the wretched gospel of the hour,
That the Ideal is secondary !

STIVER.

No !
It's primary : appointed, like the flower,
To generate the fruit, and then to go.

[*Indoors, Miss Jay plays and sings: "In the Gloaming." Stiver stands listening in silent emotion.*

With the same melody she calls me yet
Which thrilled me to the heart when first we met.

[*Lays his hand on Falk's arm and gazes intently at him.*

Oft as she wakens those pathetic notes,
From the white keys reverberating floats
An echo of the "yes" that made her mine.
And when our passions shall one day decline,
To live again as friendship, to the last
That song shall link that present to this past.
And what tho' at the desk my back grow round,
And my day's work a battle for mere bread,
Yet joy will lead me homeward, where the dead
Enchantment will be born again in sound.
If one poor bit of evening we can claim,
I shall come off undamaged from the game!

[*He goes into the house. Falk turns towards the summer-house. Svanhild comes out, she is pale and agitated. They gaze at each other in silence a moment, and fling themselves impetuously into each other's arms.*

FALK.

O, Svanhild, let us battle side by side!
Thou fresh glad blossom flowering by the tomb,—
See what the life is that they call youth's bloom!
There's coffin-stench of bridegroom and of bride;
There's coffin-stench wherever two go by
At the street corner, smiling outwardly,
With falsehood's reeking sepulchre beneath,

And in their blood the apathy of death.
And this they think is living! Heaven and earth,
Is such a load so many antics worth?
For such an end to haul up babes in shoals,
To pamper them with honesty and reason,
To feed them fat with faith one sorry season,
For service, after killing-day, as souls?

SVANHILD.

Falk, let us travel!

FALK.

Travel? Whither, then?
Is not the whole world everywhere the same?
And does not Truth's own mirror in its frame
Lie equally to all the sons of men?
No, we will stay and watch the merry game,
The conjurer's trick, the tragi-comedy
Of liars that are dupes of their own lie;
Stiver and Lind, the Parson and his dame,
See them,—prize oxen harness'd to love's yoke,
And yet at bottom very decent folk!
Each wears for others and himself a mask,
Yet one too innocent to take to task;
Each one, a stranded sailor on a wreck,
Counts himself happy as the gods in heaven;
Each his own hand from Paradise has driven,
Then, splash! into the sulphur to the neck!
But none has any inkling where he lies,
Each thinks himself a knight of Paradise,
And each sits smiling between howl and howl;
And if the Fiend come by with jeer and growl,

With horns, and hoofs, and things yet more abhorred,—
Then each man jogs the neighbour at his jowl:
"Off with your hat, man! See, there goes the Lord!"

SVANHILD (*after a brief thoughtful silence*).

How marvellous a love my steps has led
To this sweet trysting place! My life that sped
In frolic and fantastic visions gay,
Henceforth shall grow one ceaseless working day!
O God! I wandered groping,—all was dim:
Thou gavest me light—and I discovered *him!*
[*Gazing at Falk in love and wonder.*
Whence is that strength of thine, thou mighty tree
That stand'st unshaken in the wind-wrecked wood,
That stand'st alone, and yet canst shelter *me*—?

FALK.

God's truth, my Svanhild;—that gives fortitude.

SVANHILD (*with a shy glance towards the house*).

They came like tempters, evilly inclined,
Each spokesman for his half of humankind,
One asking: How can true love reach its goal
When riches' leaden weight subdues the soul?
The other asking: How can true love speed
When life's a battle to the death with Need?
O horrible!—to bid the world receive
That teaching as the truth, and yet to live!

FALK.

How if 'twere meant for us?

SVANHILD.

For us ?—What, then ?
Can outward fate control the wills of men ?
I have already said : if thou'lt stand fast,
I'll dare and suffer by thee to the last.
How light to listen to the gospel's voice,
To leave one's home behind, to weep, rejoice,
And take with God the husband of one's choice !

FALK (*embracing her*).

Come then, and blow thy worst, thou winter weather !
We stand unshaken, for we stand together !

[*Mrs Halm and Guldstad come in from the right in the background.*

GULDSTAD (*aside*).

Observe !

[*Falk and Svanhild remain standing by the summer-house.*

MRS HALM (*surprised*).

Together !

GULDSTAD.

Do you doubt it now ?

MRS HALM.

This is most singular.

GULDSTAD.

O, I've noted how
His work of late absorb'd his interest.

MRS HALM (*to herself*).

Who would have fancied Svanhild was so sly?

[*Vivaciously to Guldstad.*

But no—I can't think.

GULDSTAD.

Put it to the test.

MRS HALM.

Now, on the spot?

GULDSTAD.

Yes, and decisively!

MRS HALM (*giving him her hand*).

God's blessing with you!

GULDSTAD (*gravely*).

Thanks, it may bestead.

[*Comes to the front.*

MRS HALM

(*Looking back as she goes towards the house*).

Whichever way it goes, my child is sped.

[*Goes in.*

GULDSTAD (*approaching Falk*).

It's late, I think?

FALK.

Ten minutes and I go.

GULDSTAD.

Sufficient for my purpose.

SVANHILD (*going*).

Farewell.

GULDSTAD.

No,
Remain.

SVANHILD.

Shall I?

GULDSTAD.

Until you've answered me.
It's time we squared accounts. It's time we three
Talked out for once together from the heart.

FALK (*taken aback*).

We three?

GULDSTAD.

Yes,—all disguises flung apart.

FALK (*suppressing a smile*).

O, at your service.

GULDSTAD.

Very good, then hear.
We've been acquainted now for half a year;
We've wrangled—

FALK.

Yes.

GULDSTAD.

We've been in constant feud;
We've changed hard blows enough. You fought—alone—
For a sublime ideal; I as one
Among the money-grubbing multitude.
And yet it seemed as if a chord united
Us two, as if a thousand thoughts that lay
Deep in my own youth's memory benighted
Had started at your bidding into day.
Yes, I amaze you. But this hair grey-sprinkled
Once fluttered brown in spring-time, and this brow,
Which daily occupation moistens now
With sweat of labour, was not always wrinkled.
Enough; I am a man of business, hence—

FALK (*with gentle sarcasm*).

You are the type of practical good sense.

GULDSTAD.

And you are hope's own singer young and fain.
[*Stepping between them.*
Just therefore, Falk and Svanhild, I am here.
Now let us talk, then; for the hour is near
Which brings good hap or sorrow in its train.

FALK (*in suspense*).

Speak, then!

GULDSTAD (*smiling*).

My ground is, as I said last night,
A kind of poetry—

FALK.

In practice.

GULDSTAD (*nodding slowly*).

Right!

FALK.

And if one asked the source from which you drew— ?

GULDSTAD

(*Glancing a moment at Svanhild, and then turning again to Falk*).

A common source discovered by us two.

SVANHILD.

Now I must go.

GULDSTAD.

No, wait till I conclude.
I should not ask so much of others. You,
Svanhild, I've learnt to fathom thro' and thro';
You are too sensible to play the prude.
I watched expand, unfold, your little life;
A perfect woman I divined within you,
But long I only saw a daughter in you;—
Now I ask of you—will you be my wife?

[*Svanhild draws back in embarrassment.*

FALK (*seizing his arm*).

Hold!

GULDSTAD.

Patience; she must answer. Put your own
Question;—then her decision will be free.

FALK.

I—do you say?

GULDSTAD (*looking steadily at him*).

The happiness of three
Lives is at stake to-day,—not mine alone.
Don't fancy it concerns you less than me;
For tho' base matter is my chosen sphere,
Yet nature made me something of a seer.
Yes, Falk, you love her. Gladly, I confess,
I saw your young love bursting into flower.
But this young passion, with its lawless power,
May be the ruin of her happiness.

FALK (*firing up*).

You have the face to say so?

GULDSTAD (*quietly*).

Years give right.
Say now you won her—

FALK (*defiantly*).

And what then?

GULDSTAD (*slowly and emphatically*).

Yes, say
She ventured in one bottom to embark
Her *all*, her all upon one card to play,—
And then life's tempest swept the ship away,
And the flower faded as the day grew dark?

FALK (*involuntarily*).

She must not!

GULDSTAD (*looking at him with meaning*).

Hm. So I myself decided
When I was young, like you. In days of old
I was afire for one. Our paths divided.
Last night we met again ;—the fire was cold.

FALK.

Last night?

GULDSTAD.

Last night. You know the parson's dame—

FALK.

What? It was *she*, then, who—

GULDSTAD.

Who lit the flame.
Long I remembered her with keen regret,
And still in my remembrance she arose
As the young lovely woman that she was
When in life's buoyant spring-time first we met.
And that same foolish fire you now are fain
To light, that game of hazard you would dare.
See, that is why I call to you—beware !
The game is perilous ! Pause, and think again !

FALK.

No, to the whole tea-caucus I declared
My fixed and unassailable belief—

GULDSTAD (*completing his sentence*).

That heartfelt love can weather unimpaired

Custom, and Poverty, and Age, and Grief.
Well, say it be so ; possibly you're right ;
But see the matter in another light.
What *love* is, no man ever told us—whence
It issues, that ecstatic confidence
That one life may fulfil itself in two,—
To this no mortal ever found the clue.
But *marriage* is a practical concern,
As also is betrothal, my good sir—
And by experience easily we learn
That we are fitted just for *her*, or *her*.
But love, you know, goes blindly to its fate,
Chooses a woman, not a wife, for mate ;
And what if now this chosen woman was
No wife for you— ?

FALK (*in suspense*).

Well ?

GULDSTAD (*shrugging his shoulders*).

Then you've lost your cause.
To make a happy bridegroom and a bride
Demands not love alone, but much beside,
Relations one can meet with satisfaction,
Ideas that do not wholly disagree.
And marriage ? Why, it is a very sea
Of claims and calls, of taxing and exaction,
Whose bearing upon love is very small.
Here mild domestic virtues are demanded,
A kitchen soul, inventive and neat handed,
Making no claims, and executing all ;—
And much which in a lady's presence I
Can hardly with decorum specify.

FALK.

And therefore— ?

GULDSTAD.

Hear a golden counsel then.
Use your experience ; watch your fellow-men,
How every loving couple struts and swaggers
Like millionaires among a world of beggars.
They scamper to the altar, lad and lass,
They make a home and, drunk with exaltation,
Dwell for awhile within its walls of glass.
Then comes the day of reckoning ;—out, alas,
They're bankrupt, and their house in liquidation !
Bankrupt the bloom of youth on woman's brow,
Bankrupt the flower of passion in her breast,
Bankrupt the husband's battle-ardour now,
Bankrupt each spark of passion he possessed.
Bankrupt the whole estate, below, above,—
And yet this broken pair were once confessed
A first-class house in all the wares of love !

FALK (*vehemently*).

That is a lie !

GULDSTAD (*unmoved*).

Some hours ago 'twas true
However. I have only quoted you ;—
In these same words you challenged to the field
The "caucus" with love's name upon your shield.
Then rang repudiation fast and thick
From all directions, as from you at present ;
Incredible, I know ; who finds it pleasant

To hear the name of death when he is sick?
Look at the priest! A painter and composer
Of taste and spirit when he wooed his bride;—
What wonder if the man became a proser
When she was snugly settled by his side?
To be his lady-love she was most fit;
To be his wife, tho'—not a bit of it.
And then the clerk, who once wrote clever numbers?
No sooner was the gallant plighted, fixed,
Than all his rhymes ran counter and got mixed;
And now his Muse continuously slumbers,
Lullabied by the law's eternal hum.
Thus you see— [*Looks at Svanhild.*
Are you cold?

SVANHILD (*softly*).

No.

FALK (*with forced humour*).

Since the sum
Works out a *minus* then in every case
And never shows a *plus,*—why should you be
So resolute your capital to place
In such a questionable lottery?
It almost looks as if you fancied Fate
Had meant you for a bankrupt from your birth?

GULDSTAD (*looks at him, smiles, and shakes his head*).

My bold young Falk, reserve a while your mirth.—
There are two ways of founding an estate.
It may be built on credit—drafts long-dated
On pleasure in a never-ending bout,
On perpetuity of youth unbated,

And permanent postponement of the gout.
It may be built on lips of rosy red,
On sparkling eyes and locks of flowing gold,
On trust these glories never will be shed,
Nor the dread hour of periwigs be tolled.
It may be built on thoughts that glow and quiver,—
Flowers blowing in the sandy wilderness,—
On hearts that, to the end of life, for ever
Throb with the passion of the primal "yes."
To dealings such as this the world extends
One epithet: 'tis known as "humbug," friends.

FALK.

I see, you are a dangerous attorney,
You—well-to-do, a millionaire may-be;
While two broad backs could carry in one journey
All that beneath the sun belongs to me.

GULDSTAD (*sharply*).

What do you mean?

FALK.

That is not hard to see:
For the sound way of building, I suppose,
Is just with cash—the wonder-working paint
That round the widow's batten'd forehead throws
The aureole of a young adored saint.

GULDSTAD.

O no, tis something better that I meant.
'Tis the still flow of generous esteem,
Which no less honours the recipient

Than does young rapture's giddy-whirling dream.
It is the feeling of the blessedness
Of service, and home quiet, and tender ties,
The joy of mutual self-sacrifice,
Of keeping watch lest any stone distress
Her footsteps wheresoe'er her pathway lies;
It is the healing arm of a true friend,
The manly muscle that no burdens bend,
The constancy no length of years decays,
The arm that stoutly lifts and firmly stays.
This, Svanhild, is the contribution I
Bring to your fortune's fabric: now, reply.

[*Svanhild makes an effort to speak; Guldstad lifts his hand to check her.*

Consider well before you give your voice!
With clear deliberation make your choice.

FALK.

And how have you discovered—

GULDSTAD.

That you love her?
That in your eyes 'twas easy to discover.
Let her too know it. [*Presses his hand.*
Now I will go in.
Let the jest cease and earnest work begin;
And if you undertake that till the end
You'll be to her no less a faithful friend,
A staff to lean on, and a help in need,
Than I can be— [*Turning to Svanhild.*
Why, good, my offer's nought;

Cancel it from the tables of your thought.
Then it is I who triumph in very deed;
You're happy, and for nothing else I fought. [*To Falk.*
And, apropos—just now you spoke of cash,
Trust me, 'tis little more than tinsell'd trash.
I have no ties, stand perfectly alone;
To you I will make over all I own;
My daughter she shall be, and you my son.
You know I have a business by the border:
There I'll retire, you set your home in order,
And we'll foregather when a year is gone.
Now, Falk, you know me; with the same precision
Observe yourself: the voyage down life's stream,
Remember, is no pastime and no dream.
Now, in the name of God—make your decision!

[*Goes into the house. Pause. Falk and Svanhild look shyly at each other.*

FALK.

You are so pale.

SVANHILD.

And you so silent.

FALK.

True.

SVANHILD.

He smote us hardest.

FALK (*to himself*).

Stole my armour, too.

SVANHILD.

What blows he struck!

FALK.

He knew to place them well.

SVANHILD.

All seemed to go to pieces where they fell.
[*Coming nearer to him.*
How rich in one another's wealth before
We were, when all had left us in despite,
And Thought rose upward like the echoing roar
Of breakers in the silence of the night.
With exultation then we faced the fray,
And confidence that Love is lord of death;—
He came with worldly cunning, stole our faith,
Sowed doubt,—and all the glory pass'd away!

FALK (*with wild vehemence*).

Tear, tear it from thy memory! All his talk
Was true for others, but for us a lie!

SVANHILD (*slowly shaking her head*).

The golden grain, hail-stricken on its stalk,
Will never more wave wanton to the sky.

FALK (*with an outburst of anguish*).

Yes, we two, Svanhild—!

SVANHILD.

Hence with hopes that snare!
If you sow falsehood, you must reap despair.

For others true, you say? And do you doubt
That each of them, like us, is sure, alike,
That he's the man the lightning will not strike,
And no avenging thunder will find out,
Whom the blue storm-cloud, scudding up the sky
On wings of tempest, never can come nigh?

FALK.

The others split their souls on scattered ends:
Thy single love my being comprehends.
They're hoarse with yelling in life's Babel din:
I in this quiet shelter fold thee in.

SVANHILD.

But if love, notwithstanding, should decay,
—Love being Happiness's single stay—
Could you avert, then, Happiness's fall?

FALK.

No, my love's ruin were the wreck of all.

SVANHILD.

And can you promise me before the Lord
That it will last, not drooping like the flower,
But smell as sweet as now till life's last hour?

FALK (*after a short pause*).

It will last long.

SVANHILD (*with anguish*).

"Long!" "Long!"—Poor starveling word!
Can "long" give any comfort in Love's need?

It is her death-doom, blight upon her seed.
" My faith is, Love will never pass away"—
That song must cease, and in its stead be heard:
" My faith is, that I loved you yesterday!"

[*As uplifted by inspiration.*

No, no, not thus our day of bliss shall wane,
Flag drearily to west in clouds and rain;—
But at high noontide, when it is most bright,
Plunge sudden, like a meteor, into night!

FALK (*in anguish*).

What would you, Svanhild?

SVANHILD.

We are of the Spring;
No Autumn shall come after, when the bird
Of music in thy breast shall not be heard,
And long not thither where it first took wing.
Nor ever Winter shall his snowy shroud
Lay on the clay-cold body of our bliss;—
This Love of ours, ardent and glad and proud,
Pure of disease's taint and age's cloud,
Shall die the young and glorious thing it is!

FALK (*in deep pain*).

And far from thee—what would be left of life?

SVANHILD.

And near me what were left—if Love depart?

FALK.

A home!

SVANHILD.

Where Joy would gasp in mortal strife.

[*Firmly.*

It was not given to me to be your wife.
That is the clear conviction of my heart!
In courtship's merry pastime I can lead,
But not sustain your spirit in its need.

[*Nearer and with gathering fire.*

Now we have revell'd out a feast of spring;
No thought of slumber's sluggard couch come nigh!
Let Joy amid delirious song make wing
And flock with choirs of cherubim on high.
And tho' the vessel of our fate capsize,
One plank yet breasts the waters, strong to save;—
The fearless swimmer reaches Paradise!
Let Joy go down into his watery grave;
Our Love shall yet in triumph, by God's hand,
Be borne from out the wreckage safe to land!

FALK.

O, I divine thee! But—to sever thus!
Now, when the portals of the world stand wide,—
When the blue spring is bending over us,
On the same day that plighted thee my bride!

SVANHILD.

Just therefore must we part. Our joy's torch fire
Will from this moment wane till it expire!
And when at last our worldly days are spent,
And face to face with our great Judge we stand,
And, as a righteous God, he shall demand

Of us the earthly treasure that he lent—
Then, Falk, we cry—past power of Grace to save—
"O Lord, we lost it going to the grave!"

FALK (*with strong resolve*).

Pluck off the ring!

SVANHILD (*with fire*).

Wilt thou?

FALK.

Now I divine!
Thus and no otherwise canst thou be mine!
As the grave opens into life's Dawn-fire,
So Love with Life may not espoused be
Till, loosed from longing and from wild desire,
It soars into the heaven of memory!
Pluck off the ring, Svanhild!

SVANHILD (*in rapture*).

My task is done!
Now I have filled thy soul with song and sun.
Forth! Now thou soarest on triumphant wings,—
Forth! Now thy Svanhild is the swan that sings!

[*Takes off the ring and presses a kiss upon it.*

To the abysmal ooze of ocean bed
Descend, my dream!—I fling thee in its stead!

[*Goes a few steps back, throws the ring into the fjord, and approaches Falk with a transfigured expression.*

Now for this earthly life I have foregone thee,—
But for the life eternal I have won thee!

FALK (*firmly*).

And now to the day's duties, each, alone.
Our paths no more will mingle. Each must wage
His warfare single-handed, without moan.
We caught the fevered frenzy of the age,
Fain without fighting to secure the spoil,
Win Sabbath ease, and shirk the six days' toil,
Tho' we are called to strive and to forego.

SVANHILD.

But not in sickness.

FALK.

No,—made strong by truth.
Our heads no penal flood will overflow;
This never-dying memory of our youth
Shall gleam against the cloud-wrack like the bow
Of promise flaming in its colours seven,—
Sign that we are in harmony with heaven.
That gleam your quiet duties shall make bright—

SVANHILD.

And speed the poet in his upward flight!

FALK.

The poet, yes; for poets all men are
Who see, thro' all their labours, mean or great,
In pulpit or in schoolroom, church or state,
The Ideal's lone beacon-splendour flame afar.
Yes, upward is my flight; the winged steed
Is saddled; I am strung for noble deed.
And now, farewell!

SVANHILD.

Farewell!

FALK (*embracing her*).

One kiss!

SVANHILD.

The last!

[*Tears herself free.*

Now I can lose thee gladly till life's past!

FALK.

Tho' quenched were all the light of earth and sky,—
The thought of light is God, and cannot die.

SVANHILD (*withdrawing towards the background*).

Farewell! [*Goes further.*

FALK.

Farewell—gladly I cry again—[*Waves his hat.*
Hurrah for love, God's glorious gift to men!

[*The door opens. Falk withdraws to the right; the younger guests come out with merry laughter.*

THE YOUNG GIRLS.

A lawn dance!

A YOUNG GIRL.

Dancing's life!

ANOTHER.

A garland spread
With dewy blossoms fresh on every head!

SEVERAL.

Yes, to the dance, the dance!

ALL.

And ne'er to bed!

[*Stiver comes out with Strawman arm in arm. Mrs Strawman and the children follow.*

STIVER.

Yes, you and I henceforward are fast friends.

STRAWMAN.

Allied in battle for our common ends.

STIVER.

When the twin forces of the State agree—

STRAWMAN.

They add to all men's—

STIVER (*hastily*).

Gains!

STRAWMAN.

And gaiety.

[*Mrs Halm, Lind, Anna, Guldstad, and Miss Jay, with the other guests, come out. All eyes are turned upon Falk and Svanhild. General amazement when they are seen standing apart.*

MISS JAY (*among the Aunts, clasping her hands*).

What! Am I awake or dreaming, pray?

LIND (*who has noticed nothing*).

I have a brother's compliments to pay.

[*He, with the other guests, approaches Falk, but starts involuntarily and steps back on looking at him.*

What is the matter with you? You're a Janus
With double face!

FALK (*smiling*).

I cry, like old Montanus,
The earth is flat, Messieurs;—my optics lied;
Flat as a pancake—are you satisfied?

[*Goes quickly out to the right.*

MISS JAY.

Refused!

THE AUNTS.

Refused!

MRS HALM.

Hush, ladies, if you please!

[*Goes across to Svanhild.*

MRS STRAWMAN (*to Strawman*).

Fancy, refused!

STRAWMAN.

It cannot be!

MISS JAY.

It is!

THE LADIES (*from mouth to mouth*).

Refused! Refused! Refused!

[*They gather in little groups about the garden.*

STIVER (*dumbfounded*).

He courting? How?

STRAWMAN.

Yes, think! He laugh'd at us, ha, ha—but now—

[*They gaze at each other speechless.*

ANNA (*to Lind*).

That's good! He was too horrid, to be sure!

LIND (*embracing her*).

Hurrah, now thou art mine, entire and whole.

[*They go outside into the garden.*

GULDSTAD (*looking back towards Svanhild*).

Something is shattered in a certain soul;
But what is yet alive in it I'll cure.

STRAWMAN (*recovering himself and embracing Stiver*).

Now then, you can be very well contented
To have your dear *fiancée* for a spouse.

STIVER.

And you complacently can see your house
With little Strawmans every year augmented.

STRAWMAN

(*Rubbing his hands with satisfaction and looking after Falk*).

Insolent fellow! Well, it served him right;—

Would all these knowing knaves were in his plight!
[*They go across in conversation; Mrs Halm approaches with Svanhild.*

MRS HALM (*aside, eagerly*).

And nothing binds you?

SVANHILD.

Nothing.

MRS HALM.

Good, you know
A daughter's duty—

SVANHILD.

Guide me, I obey.

MRS HALM.

Thanks, child. [*Pointing to Guldstad.*
He is a rich and *comme il faut*
Parti; and since there's nothing in the way—

SVANHILD.

Yes, there is one condition I require!—
To leave this place.

MRS HALM.

Precisely his desire.

SVANHILD.

And time—

MRS HALM.

How long? Bethink you, fortune's calling!

SVANHILD (*with a quiet smile*).

Only a little; till the leaves are falling.

[*She goes towards the verandah; Mrs Halm seeks out Guldstad.*

STRAWMAN (*among the guests*).

One lesson, friends, we learn from this example!
Tho' Doubt's beleaguering forces hem us in,
Yet Truth upon the Serpent's head shall trample,
The cause of Love shall win—

GUESTS.

Yes, Love shall win!

[*They embrace and kiss, pair by pair. Outside to the left are heard song and laughter.*

MISS JAY.

What can this mean?

ANNA.

The students!

LIND.

The quartette,
Bound for the mountains;—and I quite forgot
To tell them—

[*The Students come in to the left and remain standing at the entrance.*

A STUDENT (*to Lind*).

Here we are upon the spot!

MRS HALM.

It's Lind you seek, then?

MISS JAY.

That's unfortunate.

He's just engaged—

AN AUNT.

And so, you may be sure,

He cannot think of going on a tour.

THE STUDENTS.

Engaged!

ALL THE STUDENTS.

Congratulations!

LIND (*to his comrades*).

Thanks, my friends!

THE STUDENT (*to his comrades*).

There goes our whole fish-kettle in the fire!
Our tenor lost! No possible amends!

FALK

(*Coming from the right, in summer suit, with student's cap, knapsack and stick*).

I'll sing the tenor in young Norway's choir!

THE STUDENTS.

You, Falk! hurrah!

FALK.

Forth to the mountains, come!
As the bee hurries from her winter home!
A twofold music in my breast I bear,
A cither with diversely sounding strings,
One for life's joy, a treble loud and clear,
And one deep note that quivers as it sings.

[*To individuals among the students.*

You have the palette?—You the note-book? Good,
Swarm then, my bees, into the leafy wood,
Till at night-fall with pollen-laden thigh,
Home to our mighty mother-queen we fly!

[*Turning to the company, while the students depart and the Chorus of the First Act is faintly heard outside.*

Forgive me my offences great and small,
I resent nothing;—

[*Softly.*

but remember all.

STRAWMAN (*beaming with happiness*).

Now fortune's garden once again is green!
My wife has hopes,—a sweet presentiment—

[*Draws him whispering apart.*

She lately whispered of a glad event—

[*Inaudible words intervene.*

If all goes well . . . at Michaelmas . . . thirteen!

STIVER

[*With Miss Jay on his arm, turning to Falk, smiles triumphantly, and says, pointing to Strawman:*

I'm going to start a household, flush of pelf!

MISS JAY (*with an ironical curtsey*).

I shall put on my wedding-ring next Yule.

ANNA (*similarly, as she takes Lind's arm*).

My Lind will stay, the Church can mind itself—

LIND (*hiding his embarrassment*).

And seek an opening in a ladies' school.

MRS HALM.

I cultivate my Anna's capabilities—

GULDSTAD (*gravely*).

An unromantic poem I mean to make
Of one who only lives for duty's sake.

FALK (*with a smile to the whole company*).

I go to scale the Future's possibilities!
Farewell!

[*Softly to Svanhild.*

God bless thee, bride of my life's dawn,
Where'er I be, to nobler deed thou'lt wake me.

[*Waves his hat and follows the Students.*

SVANHILD

[*Looks after him a moment, then says, softly but firmly:*

Now over is my life, by lea and lawn,
The leaves are falling;—now the world may take me.

[*At this moment the piano strikes up a dance, and champagne corks explode in the background. The gentlemen hurry to and fro with their ladies on their arms. Guldstad approaches Svanhild and bows: she starts momentarily, then collects herself and gives him her hand. Mrs Halm and her family, who have watched the scene in suspense, throng about them with expressions of rapture, which are overpowered by the music and the merriment of the dancers in the garden.*

[*But from the country the following chorus rings loud and defiant through the dance music:*

CHORUS OF FALK AND THE STUDENTS.

And what if I shattered my roaming bark,
It was passing sweet to be roaming!

MOST OF THE COMPANY.

Hurrah!

[*Dance and merriment; the curtain falls.*

NOTES

P. 18. "*William Russel.*" An original historic tragedy, founded upon the career of the ill-fated Lord William Russell, by Andreas Munch, cousin of the historian P. A. Munch. It was produced at Christiania in 1857, the year of Ibsen's return from Bergen, and reviewed by him in the *Illustreret Nyhedsblad* for that year, Nos. 51 and 52. Professor Johan Storm of Christiania, to whose kindness I owe these particulars, adds that "it is rather a fine play and created a certain sensation in its time; but Munch is forgotten."

P. 20. *A grey old stager.* Ibsen's friend P. Botten-Hansen, author of the play *Hyldrebryllupet.*

P. 59. *A Svanhild like the old.* In the tale of the Völsungs Svanhild was the daughter of Sigurd and Gudrun,—the Siegfried and Kriemhild of the *Nibelungenlied.* The fierce king Jormunrek, hearing of her matchless beauty, sends his son Randwer to woo her in his name. Randwer is, however, induced to woo her in his own, and the girl approves. Jormunrek thereupon causes Randwer to be arrested and hanged, and meeting with Svanhild, as he and his men ride home from the hunt, tramples her to death under their horses' hoofs. Gudrun incites her sons Sorli and Hamdir to avenge their sister; they boldly enter Jormunrek's hall, and succeed in cutting off his hands and feet, but are themselves slain by his men. This last dramatic episode is told in the Eddic *Hamthismol.*

P. 94. *In the remotest east there grows a plant.* The germ of the famous tea-simile is due to Fru Collett's romance, "The Official's Daughters" (*cf.* Introduction, p. ix.). But she exploits the idea only under a single and obvious aspect, viz. the comparison of the tender bloom of love with the precious firstling blade which brews the quintessential tea for the Chinese emperor's table; what the world calls love being, like what it calls tea, a coarse and flavourless after-crop.

NOTES

Ibsen has, it will be seen, given a number of ingenious developments to the analogy. I know Fru Collett's work only through the accounts of it given by Brandes and Jæger.

P. 135. *Another Burns.* In the original: "Dölen" ("The Dalesman"), that is A. O. Vinje, Ibsen's friend and literary comrade, editor of the journal so-called and hence known familiarly by its name. See the Introduction.

P. 160. *Like Old Montanus.* The hero of Holberg's comedy *Erasmus Montanus*, who returns from foreign travel to his native parish with the discovery that the world is *not* flat. Public indignation is aroused, and Montanus finds it expedient to announce that his eyes had deceived him, that "the world *is* flat, gentlemen."

Also from Benediction Books ...

Wandering Between Two Worlds: Essays on Faith and Art
Anita Mathias
Benediction Books, 2007
152 pages
ISBN: 0955373700

Available from www.amazon.com, www.amazon.co.uk
www.wanderingbetweentwoworlds.com

In these wide-ranging lyrical essays, Anita Mathias writes, in lush, lovely prose, of her naughty Catholic childhood in Jamshedpur, India; her large, eccentric family in Mangalore, a sea-coast town converted by the Portuguese in the sixteenth century; her rebellion and atheism as a teenager in her Himalayan boarding school, run by German missionary nuns, St. Mary's Convent, Nainital; and her abrupt religious conversion after which she entered Mother Teresa's convent in Calcutta as a novice. Later rich, elegant essays explore the dualities of her life as a writer, mother, and Christian in the United States--Domesticity and Art, Writing and Prayer, and the experience of being "an alien and stranger" as an immigrant in America, sensing the need for roots.

About the Author

Anita Mathias was born in India, has a B.A. and M.A. in English from Somerville College, Oxford University and an M.A. in Creative Writing from the Ohio State University. Her essays have been published in The Washington Post, The London Magazine, The Virginia Quarterly Review, Commonweal, Notre Dame Magazine, America, The Christian Century, Religion Online, The Southwest Review, Contemporary Literary Criticism, New Letters, The Journal, and two of HarperSanFrancisco's The Best Spiritual Writing anthologies. Her non-fiction has won fellowships from The National Endowment for the Arts; The Minnesota State Arts Board; The Jerome Foundation, The Vermont Studio Center; The Virginia Centre for the Creative Arts, and the First Prize for the Best General Interest Article from the Catholic Press Association of the United States and Canada. Anita has taught Creative Writing at the College of William and Mary, and now lives and writes in Oxford, England.

CPSIA information can be obtained at www.ICGtesting.com
Printed in the USA
LVOW131838210613

339728LV00004B/588/P